The Grandparent Solution

The Grandparent Solution

How Parents Can Build a Family Team for Practical, Emotional, and Financial Success

Arthur Kornhaber, M.D.

Foundation for
Grandparenting

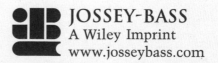

JOSSEY-BASS
A Wiley Imprint
www.josseybass.com

Published by Jossey-Bass
A Wiley Imprint
989 Market Street, San Francisco, CA 94103-1741   www.josseybass.com

Jossey-Bass books and products are available through most bookstores. To contact Jossey-Bass directly call our Customer Care Department within the U.S. at 800-956-7739, outside the U.S. at 317-572-3986, or fax 317-572-4002.

Jossey-Bass also publishes its books in a variety of electronic formats. Some content that appears in print may not be available in electronic books.

Library of Congress Cataloging-in-Publication Data
Kornhaber, Arthur.
  The grandparent solution : how parents can build a family team for practical, emotional, and financial success / Arthur Kornhaber.— 1st ed.
     p. cm.
Includes bibliographical references and index.
  ISBN 0-7879-7115-4 (alk. paper)
  1. Family. 2. Parent and adult child. 3. Grandparents. I. Title.
  HQ734.K682 2004
  306.85—dc21

                                                        2003013866

Printed in the United States of America
FIRST EDITION
PB Printing   10 9 8 7 6 5 4 3 2 1

Contents

Part Three: Grandparent Solutions

The Grandparent Solution

To my dear family

Introduction: Help Wanted

If you are like most parents today, you are probably over-worked, overextended, underfinanced, frazzled about running your child here and there for lessons and errands and games, and you don't have much time for personal reflection, romance, or even a vacation. Why do we live such frenzied lives? The answer is simple. We believe that we must do everything by ourselves and go it alone. Consequently, most of us have trapped ourselves by trying to simultaneously fulfill the goals of being a good parent, putting bread on the table, attending to family obligations, keeping up with society, trying to eke out a bit of time for personal self-expression, and more. For single parents, it is an even bigger stretch.

The tragedy is that we do not realize that we don't have to do it all ourselves, nor do we have to go it alone at all. There is a better way to structure and manage our family life. The help that most of us need is no further away than a phone call to our parents or in-laws. When we need help, we have a natural family hot line. It's 1-800-grandparents!

"What?" you might say. "My parents! Are you kidding? I don't get along with them," or "They live a thousand miles away," or "I wouldn't let my in-laws near my kid, never mind ask for help," or

"They are too busy with their own lives," or "My parents raised me and did a pretty poor job of it too," or "My parents raised me. They paid their dues, I want them to enjoy their lives now. I don't want to bother them. I should be able to handle things by myself."

However you respond, let me remind you that it is the people who raised us—our own parents, and our child's grandparents—who are uniquely positioned to help us when we need help.

Sounds great, but what's the catch? The catch is that most of us don't view grandparents as a powerful source of support. As much as we may respect grandparents—and what they do with our children—most of us do not consider them as folks who can help us manage our lives better. One reason is that we think of family in *nuclear*—that is, *two-generational* (child and parent)—terms. Many of us spend major time and energy to become "independent" from our parents and to be "autonomous" people. As a result, the idea of "grandparent help," or contemplating a "grandparent solution" for any dilemma we face, doesn't automatically pop into our minds. So we bite our tongues and bear all of our burdens alone or turn to paid strangers for assistance.

Another reason is that we are afraid to confront the difficulties of our past relationships with our parents. We therefore keep them at arm's length. This notion ignores the fact that we have grown and changed over the years and are more competent than ever before, as adults, to deal effectively with our parents.

I can safely state that with time, effort, and education we are able, with proper information and skills, to resolve most past and present conflicts with our parents. At the least, we can make enough positive changes to include them in our lives in one meaningful way or another.

Once old conflicts are resolved, grandparent support and involvement are there for the asking. Most of our parents—now older and wiser as grandparents—are waiting in the family wings to love, care, and look after us if we ask. After all, isn't that what parents do for their children all through their lifetime? Isn't that what we will do for our own? Who said we ever stop parenting our children? Allow me to elaborate.

Parents Are Parents Forever

It is an incontestable fact that when we become parents, we become parents forever. Similarly, we are children to our own parents everlastingly as well. In other words, as parents and children, we are connected forever: present, past, and future.

It is also a fact that no matter how old we are, *we never stop needing our parents*. Equally, our parents, no matter how old they are, never stop needing us. This need-satisfaction equation binds us from the day we are born, to the day we have our first child, to the day we die. As soon as our first child is born, we begin to worry about its health and well-being. This concern lasts forever, whether we are thirty years old or eighty years old and whether we want to acknowledge it or not. How we love, nurture, and provide for our child shifts and changes seamlessly throughout our lifetimes, and the same holds true for our child. Over the years, change, growth, and learning occur simultaneously, in often bittersweet mirror images of one another: the first steps of a child are away from the parent.

Even today, our living parents still worry about us in the same way that we worry about our child. Some cultures and religious belief systems hold that this concern continues after earthly life. True or not, it gives us something to think about. One thing that we know for sure is that our parents resonate emotionally, biologically, and spiritually to our state of well-being and material circumstances. They are tuned in to our needs (as every parent who has spent a sleepless night worrying about a child knows well). This happens whether we get along with one another or not, whether we live near or far from one another, and whatever our age. Whether seen or unseen, expressed or unexpressed, this *vital connection* is always turned on.

That is why we should take advantage of this truth and create a family arrangement with a philosophy and structure that makes use of our parents, as our child's grandparents. We have it in our hands to create a family arrangement that assures us that we will no longer have to go it alone—an arrangement that offers the possibility of any help and support we may need, whenever we need it. And, I might mention, often free of charge. I call this kind of setup a *family team*. I feel that this is the best of all family arrangements. Here's why.

Transforming Parents into Grandparents

The family team is a natural structure. When we become parents, a radical change in our family's generational boundaries takes place. The birth of our child seamlessly transforms our parents into grandparents. This event adds a brand new generation to our family configuration—the former child becomes a parent, and the former parent becomes a grandparent. With the new addition, the family becomes *three-generational: child-parent-grandparent*. By arranging the generations in such a sequential manner, Mother Nature supplies us with all the players on the family team.

Over time, these succeeding generations move up the generational ladder, ensuring that each new generation profits from the experience and support of all who came before. Equally, this system supplies an emotional and spiritual protective haven in which all three generations—child, parent, and grandparent—can complement one another's needs, provide mutual support, and grow together. Most important, the family team is the only system that includes grandparents, thereby making them available to help children and parents when needed. Those who go it alone, in a two-generational nuclear family, have no involved grandparents available for help.

Of course, this family team idea is nothing new. It just gives a name to the way that nature structures a template in which to live family life. The problem is that we have lost touch with this excellent way of structuring and managing our family. What we need to do then is to find a way to adapt and apply this form to today's times. If we can do this successfully, we will no longer have to go it alone, and neither will our children.

Understanding the Rites of Passage

When our child first comes along, we take on the privilege and responsibility of parenthood with a pledge to love and care for our child forever. Our own parents, as grandparents, have new privileges and responsibilities too. At the same time that they continue to provide for us as parents, they now to have to deal with our sacred and beautiful gift to them—their new, adorable grandchild.

Now that we have become parents, and our family dynamics have changed, our parents need to recognize our major rite of passage, encourage and support us as parents, respect our new generational boundaries, and expand the way they view us. Moreover they need to understand the changes within themselves as grandparents and of course to have a great time with their new grandchild.

They also have to expand their parenting role with us by making themselves available to help us both directly and indirectly when it concerns our child. Love, help, and commitment go both ways of course. In the best of all worlds, our parents care for us, and eventually, we care for them. When we get old, our child will care for us. And so on down the line. What goes around comes around. A strong and committed family team supplies the place for this to happen.

Parents as the Central Command

Viewing our family from a structural point of view, we find ourselves, as parents, positioned at the fulcrum of the natural three-dimensional family structure. Our child is on one side, grandparents on the other. From this pivotal location, we have maximum perspective and are positioned to see the needs of others.

Because we are at the center of things, we are also empowered with the natural authority to manage the entire system and ensure effective communication between the parties. Simply put, we occupy the central command post of our family team. When we understand and apply these conditions to the fullest—perspective, authority, and command—we become what I call a *three-dimensional parent*. In this role, we have a clear sense of the family team, perspective, authority, command, and communication. We help everyone understand their role and their place and help members contribute to family joy, health, and harmony. In addition, as a three-dimensional parent, we recognize the value and power of our own parents and respect their place on the family team. By so doing, we may use them in a variety of ways to accentuate the positive and eliminate the negative in our family's life.

Seeing the Forest

I present the concept of three-dimensional parenting and the family team as an ideal for all of us to strive for. I have learned the value of this model during years of clinical experience. I have especially learned a great deal from the many young children I have worked with professionally over the years. Young children, and the very old, see life as a forest. They see the big picture of the family and the world, as an organic and benign place for them. Most of the time, the middle generations see only the trees. In fact, one of the main functions of children is to keep parents in touch with the wonder of the forest. I have come to respect young children as true family experts. Through conversation, play, drawings, and more, I have learned that they see the world in a clear, truthful, down-to-earth, and organic way that supplies a blueprint for a happy family. I have called these qualities the *oracular* ability of the child (referring to the innate wisdom and clear-sightedness of a child, similar to those qualities of an *oracle*).

For most children, this clear-seeing ability begins to atrophy around the age of seven—the alleged age of reason. This happens because social influences and information (school, media, and the like) begin to flood the child's consciousness and overwhelm innate emotional and spiritual experience, meditational reflection (day-dreaming), clarity of thought, and acute observational abilities (which explains why an aging Picasso said that he would give anything if he could paint the way he did when he was a child).

So at the age of three or four, children see the world with crystal-like clarity, and at the same time, they begin to acquire the verbal ability to express their views to a respectful and understanding ear. Remember, "Kids say the darnedest (clear and truthful) things." I am often awed and flabbergasted by children's pure and clear perceptions of reality. When I asked Billy, a ten-year-old boy, to draw a picture of his family, he drew an amazing image that was a perfect representation of a three-dimensional family. Subsequently, we adapted Billy's picture as a logo for the Foundation for Grandparenting (Figure 1).

In this picture, the child sees himself supported by his parents and his grandparents. As children do, he sees his "family" as composed of generations of people, layered like a parfait, in three separate yet distinct units—child, parent, grandparent.

In the child's mind, each unit has its own place (to see what I mean, look at some old family pictures and check out who is sitting where, or ask your young child to draw a family picture). In addition, each unit is unique in its functions, possesses its own privileges and responsibilities, and occupies its own dimension of time (age). The child sees each generation differently and expects them to act differently. Yet the generations interact closely and can blend together when necessary. Each generation, in its own time, moves into the succeeding layer and maintains some of what went before. There is therefore a child and parent within every grandparent.

What is also important is how organically connected a child sees his family. When I asked Denise, nine years old, to draw a picture to represent her family, she drew a large rectangle.

FIGURE 1. Billy's Picture.

Source: Foundation for Grandparenting.

"What is this?" I asked.

"My family," she answered.

"All I see is a rectangle," I said.

"It's a box." She smiled. "The side of a box, y'know, like those boxes that start out little and get bigger and bigger and go inside of each other. That's my family. I am the big box, and my parents and grandparents and everyone are littler boxes, and they all go inside of me."

This ultimately sensible arrangement forms, in the child's eyes, a three-dimensional, basic, organic, dovetailing, natural structure for the family team. Unfortunately, times and human nature being what they are, we as adults (for reasons I will explain later) often lose sight of this natural wonder because we are too busy to pay attention.

One reason I am writing this book is to remind you of this marvel. Another is because I want you to recognize, honor, and replicate what children teach us about the "rightness" of acting and thinking three-dimensionally. Here is what they say:

1. Love and care for the child.
2. Maintain a healthy child-parent relationship with our own parents.
3. Respect and assist our parents' new grandparenting roles with our child.
4. Create, nurture, and manage a three-dimensional family.
5. Get along well!

Note that the child's blueprint for family life includes grandparents. It allows parents to access "grandparent power"—the grandparents' wisdom, experience, love, dedication, and resources. We can recruit their expertise to assist us when we need advice, counsel, judgments, and solutions. With grandparents on board, we have all of our bases covered. From our position of authority as head of our family team, we can begin to learn from present and past mistakes to right the wrongs of past generations and finally put an end to family miseries that have been transmitted through generations. By so doing, we create a better family than ever before to benefit not only our child today but our future progeny as well.

Easier Said Than Done

Stating an ideal is one thing. Making it happen is another. Of course, becoming a three-dimensional parent, life and human nature being what it is, is not easy; however, we already have some impressive qualifications to help us begin. Our life experience is one. Our voyage from childhood to parenthood has taught us much (just as the continuation of our journey to grandparenthood, and even great-grandparenthood, will teach us even more).

Most of us have already learned a great deal in the school of hard knocks. We know what we want and what we do not want. We know what works and what doesn't. We know what makes us happy and what makes us suffer. We know we want the best for our child.

In addition to our experience, we have some ready-made personnel. Nature has supplied the people we need—grandparents (perhaps great-grandparents too)—as standard biological issue to help us. How well we can use grandparents depends on our previous family history. If we have excellent relationships with grandparents, it is easy to include them on our family team. We have only to ask. If we have past or present difficulties with them, we have to heal any wounds first. For many of us, this will not be easy. We will have to undertake a major effort to change any negative attitudes before we know how to ask or what to ask of grandparents when we seek their counsel or look to them for solutions. Bad experiences in the past, emotional baggage, entrenched attitudes, as well as realistic logistics, are all challenges to overcome. It is nevertheless possible to do, and I have helped many parents do so over the years. Although lots of mental and physical effort is required, it is well worth the effort. All of us, and our children, deserve it. Unborn generations of our family will thank us.

The Emotional Power of Our Family Connections

To emphasize why this effort is so important, I would like to elaborate a bit further about why it is so psychologically, and spiritually, important to push past any negative attitudes that we may harbor toward our parents. If there has been only one thing drummed into my consciousness in over forty years of clinical practice as a child and family psychiatrist, it is this:

To derive our deepest source of satisfaction and our greatest sense of joy and meaning in life, we must ultimately learn to deal with and eventually come to terms with the people to whom we are biologically, emotionally, socially, and (in some cases) spiritually attached. That is our family of origin, which I like to call our *vital connections*.

Our vital connections influence, through both nature and nurture, every aspect of our being. They influence our personality and physical appearance through inherited genes. They affect how we behave, which is determined by how, where, and by whom we are raised. Our vital connections determine our learned historical, family-social-ethnic origins. The ephemeral, fuzzy qualities of our relationships (love, attachment) with our relatives transcend time and place. The quality of these relationships, for good or bad, influences our reason for being and our sense of personal life meaning, self-esteem, and more. Our personal experiences with our past, present, and future relatives can make us happy or miserable. Relatives can make us joyful or aggravated. They can bestow power, rapture, and delight. Or they can give us headaches, heartaches, and backaches that remain with us forever.

The emotional power of our vital connections is stronger, more pervasive, and more enduring than anything else of this world—even money. Money and fame do not last. That is because the benefits of social and material success do not penetrate to the *core of our being*. That is why young children can be happy in any environment with a loving adult. It is no matter to a child if the adult is rich or poor, old or young, or anything else. These little "oracles" intuitively know that the deepest dimensions of our *self* resonate to the quality (and the level of love) of our psychological, emotional, social, and even spiritual attachments to our blood relations.

Children die for love. Science has shown that the fatal (when untreated) infant *failure-to-thrive syndrome* is directly linked to the lack of love that a baby experiences. True emotions, a deep and enduring sense of success, comfort, satisfaction with self, enduring pleasure, meaningfulness, and usefulness are experienced in the deepest regions of our heart and soul. Human achievements that do not plumb this dimension of our being are superficial and ephemeral, lacking deep meaning and satisfaction, as evidenced by some of the saddest and most alienated, although materially well-off, patients that I have treated during my professional life. A little boy with an absent mother (who may be the president of a major corporation) wants his mother's time and essence, not the material goods that her position may purchase.

The Permanence of Family

Because our blood relationships are *always* with us, we must do the best we can with them. Like a mountain spring, the thoughts, feelings, and internal dialogue (*self-talk*—chatting with ourselves) generated by our family relationships, for better or worse, chatter continually in our unconscious minds. Often they rise into immediate awareness as a conscious thought, a fantasy, a feeling of love, anger, revenge, concern, compassion. We experience this every day.

Mothers, fathers, sisters, brothers, grandparents, children, grandchildren, and others, alive or long gone, all dance in our conscious, unconscious, or dreaming mind—permanently. Consequently, much of our self-talk concerns reliving past experiences, wishing we had done something differently, telling people off, anticipating the future, or hoping and praying for good things to happen to our loved ones. Better these conversations are loving and happy than negative and contentious.

There is no escape from our relatives. Just ask any psychotherapist.

Other Important Connections

You may be wondering how close non-blood-related relationships fit into this picture. Of course, other blood relations—brothers, sisters, aunts, and uncles—are very important. But our "acquired" relationships (other than the family of origin) can be important and profound as well. They may be friends, lovers, life partners, buddies in the next foxhole, colleagues, mentors, sports team members, kindred spirits, or spouses.

Of course, these important and valuable emotional connections add another dimension to our lives. The people involved can be important members of our family team. Indeed some of these relationships may even share many of the same dynamics as our relationships with blood relatives. But this is for another book. As far as this work is concerned, I will limit my discussion to the *three-dimensional relationship* between children, parents, and grandparents and what it means to us as *three-dimensional parents*.[1]

No Easy Ride

Now that I have made my point about the importance of family, I want to return to grim reality and the "easier-said-than-done" comment I made earlier. The idea that grandparents can offer a solution to our problems may sound great. But what if we don't like them or don't get along with them?

We all know that dealing with our relatives is like riding on an emotional roller coaster: soaring up during the good times and swooping down during the bad. Love, peace, understanding, and joy at one moment. Misunderstanding, conflict, hurt, and anger at the next. Forgiveness and reconciliation on the way up. Disappointment on the way down. Sometimes we ride alone. Other times we have company. Never a dull moment.

Of all the types of family relationships that we experience (brothers, sisters, aunts, grandparents), none has higher highs or lower lows than the *two-dimensional relationship* with our own parents (parent-child). When our child is born, or even before, our past and present relationship with our parents, and in-laws too, will influence for better or worse how much we will want them to be involved with our child. The good news is that many of the negative experiences that we suffered in the two-dimensional relationship with our parents can be resolved, forgiven, and healed when we become a three-dimensional parent.

When we have both our child and our parents to deal with, and we negotiate how they deal with one another, the possibilities for both joy and happiness become exponentially greater. There's more to consider. We must add our partner's attitudes to this mix, as well as other situational and circumstantial factors, such as changing times, attitudes and lifestyles, work, changes in marital status, and more.

The Family Law of Relativity

Being a three-dimensional parent means that we include grandparents as part of our family team. If we have a great relationship with grandparents, this is easily done. If we don't, we need to resolve and heal any past conflicts. Consider the following principle, which I call the *family law of relativity:*

When we have conflicts with relatives, get rid of the conflicts, and not the relatives.

It sounds simple, and again, it's easier to say than to do. Nevertheless I have seen many three-dimensional parents succeed at keeping their family team together in the face of enormous challenges. They resolve conflicts with family members satisfactorily and preserve them, wiser for the experience, on their family roster. Then when a need arises, they have a diversity of people to call for help. That is why it is critically important for us to understand and apply this principle to addressing and healing any current conflicts with grandparents (as I will show).

Applying this principle to our daily lives may require a change of attitude and may well be one of the toughest things we ever have to do, but as I will show later, it is more than worth the effort. We start with reexamining our attitudes and the way we conceive our family and our family life. Reflect on the *child's* view of family life, as I discussed previously. Is it similar to yours? Reflect on the following for a while:

1. *We have changed our parents' lives.* Sometimes we ignore, take for granted, and even minimize the enormousness of what takes place when we become parents. As I have pointed out, when our child is born, we launch ourselves and our own parents into another familial dimension. The act of creating a child opens the door to a new stage of life. Similarly, we catapult our own parents into a new generation, without their having a thing to say about it (although surely they are overjoyed and grateful).

2. *We are very generous.* We can be proud when we give our parents the gift of a grandchild. By so doing, we add joy as well as a new identity, meaning, and sense of value to the new grandparents' lives. That is very nice of us. Reflect for a moment on how important this is. We give our child a gift of grandparents too. We supply our child with people to love, support, and adore her in a way completely different than we do.

3. *We touch immortality.* By creating and connecting these generations, and establishing new vital connections, we perform a powerful biological function: perpetuating our family line and humanity in general. The child we create supplies us, our partner, our parents, and our partner's parents (all grandparents, and maybe great-grandparents) with a loving and eager vessel, a cute and adored receptacle into which we can safely store the treasures of our family—its past history, values, heritage, and emotional attachments. They may therefore be perpetuated into the future.

And that is not all. From the day we become parents, we begin to plant the seeds of our own future grandparenthood, and great-grandparenthood too. So when we take the time to think about it all, we have accomplished a great deal.

Assessing Your Family

Now it's time for some practical details. Although the birth of a child lays the groundwork for a potential three-dimensional family relationship, it does not happen without our attention and care. There are things we must do and family logistics to consider and work out in order to grow our family and deal with any conflicts and challenges.

We must consider our previous family experience, family history, current situation, and personal priorities. We must ask ourselves how these factors affect, for better or worse, the possibility of becoming a three-dimensional parent. For example, if we are currently locked into a nuclear family configuration, as so many of us are today, we need to determine which family members are available to us to expand our family team. Are we truly alone, or are there grandparents that we can recruit for our family team if we make the effort?

Many of us have experiences, attitudes, and ideas that may make us hesitant to involve grandparents in our lives. Some of us limit contact with grandparents because we are concerned that grandparents will repeat the same mistakes they made in raising us with our own children (although research shows that most grandparents do learn from past mistakes). Some of us proactively distance ourselves from our families of origin, and especially grandparents, because of unresolved childhood and family issues, still holding on to past anger and grudges. And at the sad extreme, but not uncommon today at all, more parents than we would imagine (whether justified or not) *permanently separate* their children from grandparents that they don't like or get along with. By so doing, many of these folks lose their own parents as well. This latter situation generates intense acrimony, so much so that parent-grandparent disputes end up in the hands of the judicial system and have generated the well-publicized *grandparents' rights* controversy that we will examine later in the book.

Normalizing Conflicts and Problems

We should not despair if we have a current family conflict with grandparents that makes us pessimistic about the possibility of creating a family team. Family problems are normal and expected.

None of us is immune. The good news is that with proper effort and skill, most are fixable. If you are a bit skeptical, perhaps this principle will help:

When conflict is present, most often it is not the problem per se that is the main challenge. It is rather how the problem is addressed, managed, and resolved.

Even though the sheer number and diversity of possible family problems borders on the infinite, there are effective ways, as I will discuss later, of addressing and dealing with them. Just to give you an idea of the scope and diversity of such issues (limited to parents and grandparents), here is a sampling of questions and problems that I have received over the years from parents who want to be closer to grandparents but who have found that conflicts got in the way. Some of the communicational disconnects, conflicts, and problems that they describe may ring a bell for you:

- My father smokes around my children. He is pigheaded, and I am afraid to tell him to stop. What can I do?

- My mother and I have had many problems over the years. To survive, I have distanced myself from her. Then I had a child. My mother is crazy about my child, and my child likes my mother (who is less critical as a grandmother than she was as a mother), but I can't stand being around her. My child knows this and it upsets her. Help!

- When my mother-in-law comes to visit, she takes over my house and my kids. She only pays attention to her son. I am treated like a second-class citizen. My three kids are crazy about her. My husband wants me to grin and bear it, but I can't. Even praying doesn't help. I need advice.

- I am a Caucasian woman who adopted an Asian child. My parents are not taking to her. I am heartbroken. What can I do to get them more involved?

- If I hear my mother say, "This is the way we did it when I was a mother" anymore, I might lose it. She makes me feel inadequate. How can I get her to respect the modern way I want to raise my son?

- My mother has certain unpleasant character traits. Is it all right to leave her alone with my children? Will my children catch her traits?

- What's so special about the grandparent-grandchild relationship? My father was a cheapskate with me when I was young, but he spends money on my kids like there is no tomorrow. What happened to him?

- I am a gay man in a committed relationship. We want to adopt a child, but my parents think I'm crazy and want nothing to do with it. I want my child to have grandparents. How can I get them to change their minds?

- My parents are completely disinterested in my children, and they feel it. Can I do anything about it?

- My husband and I work full-time. We have a two-year-old that we have to put in day care. My mother lives nearby and is retired. Yet she does not want to baby-sit my daughter on a regular basis. How can I convince her we need her?

- We have a very different lifestyle than my parents. They undermine the way we want to raise our children. Yet I don't want to separate them from my children because they are very close. What can I do?

- My parents are very intrusive people. I am very angry with them and am no longer allowing them near my children. They want to go to court to get visitation. What can I do to avoid this?

- My parents care for my child several times a week. Their rules are different from mine. I do not want my child to be confused. I don't want to hurt my parents feelings either. How do I tell them without hurting their feelings?

- I feel like my own parents are always watching over my shoulder when I am with my son. This makes me very uncomfortable and nervous with them. I do not know if it is my problem or theirs. Either way, I feel very insecure. Any advice?

How many of these problems have you personally encountered? How many have you resolved to your satisfaction? How many still fester, even continue to make trouble? The greatest help in dealing with such problems is to be found in our personal will and desire to fix the problem, and then developing the knowledge and practical skills to do so.

To be three-dimensional parents, we need to possess both motivation and the personal qualities of maturity, perspective, vision, and commitment (which you, the reader, probably already possess, or you would not be reading this book). With these qualities, and what you will learn in this book, you can elevate your *parent-consciousness* (just as your interest was piqued by reading the questions that I just shared with you). As you read on, you will heighten your introspective ability.

Your Own Experience as a Grandchild

For example, you will become more aware of what is taking place and what has taken place (past, present, and future) between you and your own parents. You might begin thinking about what changes took place when your two-dimensional relationship with your parents (child-parent, where you are the child) changed to a three-dimensional one (child-parent-grandparent, where you are the parent). You will also become more aware of the intricacies (family-wise) of what transpires between your child and you and between your child and your own parents—their complex and unique grandchild-grandparent bond—from your perch as a parent. In fact, if you review your own personal experience as a grandchild, you will gain a greater perspective of your child's experience as a grandchild, because you now share similar experiences as a grandchild.

Because our family continually grows and changes, there is something new to learn every day. Do you remember how your own parents acted with your grandparents? Did they help or hinder your relationship with them? Were you raised in a family team or in a nuclear arrangement? What has your experience as a grandchild been like? Have you personally experienced how the grandparent-grandchild bond is a direct and separate human bond, second only in emotional importance to the parent-child bond? Was your experience positive or negative? Is it similar to the joyful experience of French author Jean-Paul Sartre, who wrote that he "could make my grandmother go into raptures of joy by being hungry"?[2] Or has your experience been more dismal, like that of Sally, eight years old, who told me, "My grandmother hates me because I have too much energy and cannot sit still"? Or has it been like the experience of Levon, eleven, who is sad because he never met his grandparents?

Your answers to these questions will give you some insight about your current attitudes and perspective that you may not have previously considered and may influence your present attitudes. Do you see firsthand how the relationship between your child and his grandparents is psychologically, emotionally, and socially different from *your* parent-child relationship? Do you see these differences in action? Do you realize how very, very important *you* are as the *linchpin* between these two generations? Do you understand how deeply aware and involved that you, like a weaver, need to be as you knit your parents and your child together with yourself to create the fabric of your family?

Why This Book

Summing up, I have written this book specifically

- In recognition of how hard it is to be a parent today.
- To help you, as a parent, understand the importance of the three-dimensional view of your family: as your child, yourself, and your parents.
- To help you become a three-dimensional parent and create a strong and vibrant family team for now and for the future. By

so doing, you may be able to access grandparents for the benefit of all.

- To prompt you to review past hurts or other negative experiences with your own parents, then to use these experiences as
  information, and assess how (or if) they were resolved and
  how much the residue currently affects your behavior.

- To help you learn how to use grandparents as an effective
  resource, in a diversity of ways and circumstances, to better
  your own life.

- To teach you the skills necessary to confront and deal with
  conflicts that threaten your family team.

- To help you enhance your current relationship with
  grandparents.

- To help you proceed to positive personal change and clear out
  your emotional closet so you can forgive, forget, and move on
  to a better family life.

- To empower you to prevent and heal current or emerging
  problems: by helping you identify, understand, and both
  prevent and effectively deal with common challenges
  or more serious conflicts that you may encounter with
  grandparents.

- To help you understand and enhance your children's relationship with your parents.

- To guide you in preparing for your future and helping you be
  the best grandparent possible when your turn comes.

- To prompt you to be aware, to communicate, and to widen
  your horizons by putting you in touch with other people's
  experience through anecdotes and the sharing of information.

- To assist you in changing your own life and the lives of your
  family members for the better.

- To help you leave a wonderful legacy for those who will come
  after.

How the Book Is Organized

I have divided the book into three parts. The first part is called Vital Connections. Chapter One, Family Matters, gives you some background about the difficulties of family life today and why a better way is needed. I also introduce and explain the differences between two- and three-dimensional families and present the benefits of the three-dimensional structure.

In Chapter Two, Sticking Together, I explain the ideal three-dimensional family (team) model, why it is necessary, and how you may use it as a blueprint for constructing your own three-dimensional family.

In Chapter Three, Members of the Family Team, I show you how the three-dimensional family team works and familiarize you with what goes on emotionally between the other members of your three-dimensional family (your parents and child) and your critical role in this relationship.

To be a successful three-generational parent, we need to effectively manage our own personal relationships with both our child and our parents. Information about how we can improve our parenting skills and deal with conflicts with our children is easily found in many books, publications, and parent Web sites. Information about doing the same with our own parents is scarce. That is until now. In Part Two, Building the Family Team, I show how to identify, deal with, and resolve both expected and exceptional conflicts with grandparents.

Chapter Four, Overcoming the Past, explains the importance of identifying and correcting past child-parent conflicts that many of us have experienced at some time or other with our parents. When unresolved, such conflicts prevent us from using grandparents as effectively as possible. It is necessary to resolve these conflicts to maximize our parents' contribution to our family team.

In Chapter Five, Managing Family Conflicts, I show how conflicts occur and develop (when treated and untreated) and offer helpful guidelines that you can use to resolve them. The next four chapters deal with the specific types of conflictual situations with grandparents that many of us encounter.

Chapter Six, Personal Conflicts, deals with personality types and differences, trespassing over family boundaries, and personal narcissism (selfishness).

Chapter Seven, Situational and Circumstantial Conflicts, deals with spoiling, favoritism, discipline, competing grandparents, too much grandparenting, too little grandparenting (grandparent deprivation), and more.

Chapter Eight, Family Rearrangements, discusses divorce, remarriage, and stepfamily situations, as well as the effects of a grandparent's divorce on the family, and especially on grandchildren.

Chapter Nine, Family Diversity, addresses conflicts that occur with family diversity arising from intermarriage, adoption, remarriage, as well as race, religion, and gay and lesbian issues.

Part Three of this book, Grandparent Solutions, shows you how to proactively ask grandparents for personal help and support in a variety of emotional, financial, and other circumstances.

Chapter Ten, Asking for Practical Help, helps you understand the importance of asking grandparents for support in such situations as the birth of a child, baby-sitting, visiting, finances, living long distances from one another, and more.

Chapter Eleven, Asking for Emotional Support, expands the spectrum of grandparents' helping possibilities to circumstances that can be emotionally taxing: adoption, divorce, illness, children with special needs, even raising a child when necessary.

Using the Book

There are two ways you can use this book. Read the book straight through from beginning to end for the most thorough and far-ranging understanding of the subject. You can use it on an "emergency" basis as well. If you need some information and guidance quickly about a "hot" topic (for example, feuding grandparents, or getting grandparents to help with a special needs child, or spoiling), refer directly to the appropriate chapter. You can also use the book as a "reading" on a given topic. In this method, you and a grandparent can read a specific topic and discuss your impressions together. The purpose for this might be merely academic, of relevance to your own relationship. This is a diplomatic way for a parent to broach a sensitive topic with an "offending" grandparent.

I have also included a section on Resources, where you can find organizations, readings, Web sites, and a host of other useful material to supplement the material in this book and expand your learning on a given topic.

Personal Note

Because I am a son, grandson, husband, father, grandfather, and family psychiatrist, who has studied the child-parent-grandparent relationship for over thirty years, I could write this book from many points of view. However, I have chosen to write from a parent's point of view.

Doing so has been an enlightening experience. It is especially gratifying to recognize how much perspective and respect for everyone's special views and experience I have gained over the years. The material I present is based on my clinical experience, past and ongoing research (including a recent survey exploring parent-grandparent relationships), as well as information from parent and grandparent interviews, conversations, letters, and general inquiries involving parent-grandparent issues to the Foundation for Grandparenting (print and Web site).

In the course of my work, I have accumulated a file of clinical cases involving children, parents, and grandparents that illustrate certain clinical points or situations. I have used these cases in many of my writings on grandparenting. In this book, I revisit a few of these cases in a new and different way: this time from the parents', and sometimes the child's, viewpoint. Of course, I have altered every name, place, and situation for anonymity's sake and sometimes have combined and condensed interview material for the sake of understanding and relevance.

I am pleased to let you know that you can keep up-to-date on this subject and can even communicate with others interactively via the Parents and Grandparents section of the Foundation for Grandparenting's Web site, www.grandparenting.org. This section of the site is a forum that serves as an extension of your family team. The Web site provides a forum for parents and grandparents to share circumstances and experiences, both positive and negative, and provides a "cyberopportunity" to offer one another kind advice and helpful hints.

Creating an Enduring Legacy

I want to urge you to make an effort to create a healthy and happy three- (or four-) generational-dimensional family system for yourself and your posterity. You have before you a new and unprecedented opportunity to reinvent your family.

You have the opportunity to learn from past mistakes—applying what you already know and what you will learn from this book to your family life—so you can accentuate the positive and eliminate the negative. Based on my experience with many parents, I can state the following with some certainty: if you try hard to do the best you can with what you have to work with (however daunting that might seem at the moment), you can, at the least, improve some aspects of your family life. At the most, you can change your family life significantly for the better.

Your efforts to this end will set a powerful example for your child, who will benefit from your labors and dedication and by following your example will support your own (as well as his or her) grandparenthood in the future.

There is no greater legacy to leave your loved ones!

Acknowledgments

Every time we undertake a new endeavor with others, whether it is for love, play, work, or service, we coalesce a new family of sorts, quite different from our family of origin. This new structure may last a lifetime, as in the case of school friends, or it may disappear when the reason for coalescing evaporates. The nature of such a family profoundly influences the quality of the endeavor. This is true whether it applies to learning in a classroom, a baseball team, an army unit, a medical team, a business endeavor, or writing a book.

This book is the result of such a family effort: a new professional family—multigenerational and multidimensional—that materialized during its creation.

The grandparent role in the family was played by my wise and kind literary agent, James Levine, who provided encouragement and excellent guidance and set proper boundaries. Alan Rinzler, my creative, insightful, and excellent editor at Jossey-Bass, played the role of all-seeing, three-dimensional parents. Alan provided "unconditional" vision, wisdom, experience, direction, and perspective to the writing—keeping the family coordinated and on task. Carol Hartland, Marcy Marsh, Sachie Jones, and Jennifer Wenzel, of Jossey-Bass, played dual roles—parental in their areas of expertise in production, editing, and marketing and sibling-like when it concerned our mutual interest in baseball.

I guess I was the kid.

Thanks to all.

Arthur Kornhaber, M.D.
Ojai, California

PART ONE

Vital Connections

1

Family Matters

Yeah. Me. My parents and all my grandparents. We are one for
all and all for one.

—Alex, nine years old

    Family still matters, but it ain't like it used to be. We are con-
stantly being challenged by contemporary changes in the way we
value and view family and society, as compared with what we nor-
mally expect because of the way we were raised.

    I think it is safe to say that most of us were raised in a more
ordered and a less violent culture (even though we may have
rebelled against it in our youth) than the one we live in today. Now
that the generational tables have been turned, and we are in charge,
this enormous difference between where we are and where we came
from leaves us feeling disoriented about our own values, lives, and
priorities.

    We worry for our children as well. It can be downright nerve-
racking having to raise a child and be concerned, if not obsessed,
about pervasive and often life-threatening and demoralizing influences. You know what they are: the loss of values and ethics in society, white collar and violent crime, noxious marketing influence on
young minds, child pornography, drive-by shootings, alcohol, drugs,
perverts, and the media drumbeat about all of them.

    If dealing with "outside" toxic social influences is not enough
to worry about, the "inside"—our family itself—is being tossed on
the sea of change as well. So fast are the waves of change that the
noted anthropologist Margaret Mead alluded to the speed as "the
acceleration of history."[1] Consequently, our traditional concepts of

parenthood and family structure have been destabilized in *only one* generation. It only takes a long look around at your friends and neighbors and community to see what I mean.

For example, a traditional lifelong commitment to marriage (at least to the same person, and regardless of the quality of the bond) is no longer the norm. (Remember, "For better or worse, 'til death do us part"?) The conventional troika—mom, dad, and the kids—prevalent before the Second World War, is not the norm anymore either, nor is the traditional role of grandparents in the family. In 1950, half of American households had grandparents living in them. Today it is under 10 percent.

It is not only that family dissolution and serial marriages have become commonplace, but many people are shunning formal marriage (vows and all) and choosing to sidestep tying the knot in favor of cohabiting. Divorce and remarriage are swelling the ranks of single parents and stepparents. Single parenting by choice is on the increase. All of this can be very discombobulating for children.

At least one-quarter of children of divorced single-parent families are in shared custody and live in two households. Over 30 percent of all children live with a single parent. Since 1970, the percentage of households with children where both parents work has *tripled*. How can a parent's influence be consistent and reliable under such circumstances? Especially single parents. If family really matters, help is sorely needed.

Reinventing the Family

There is more. At the same time that traditional parenthood is undergoing deconstruction, families are being reinvented in different and unprecedented ways. Medical science, for example, is helping many aspiring parents (who were previously unsuccessful at conceiving a child in the "typical" way) achieve their dream of parenthood through in vitro fertilization and surrogates. More broadminded and tolerant social attitudes have resulted in an increase in ethnic, racial, and religious diversity in marriage. Adoptive parents are taking children of different races and religions to their hearts. Millions of gay and lesbian persons are becoming parents via birth, adoption, or surrogates, and at a prodigious rate. Who knows what is next? If cloning succeeds, future generations might be parenting cloned versions of themselves! Someone could really end up being, as the song says, their "own grandpa!"

Because of change and turmoil, we have all learned that whatever values we adhere to and whatever family arrangement we choose— married, single, divorced, remarried, gay or lesbian—and no matter how hard we try, it is impossible to meet all of our child's needs alone. Help is always required. Yet even with this knowledge that we and our child need love and support beyond what we can supply in a nuclear family, few of us today automatically "think grandparent" when it comes to filling this role. We remain stuck in a two-dimensional, nuclear family mind-set, where grandparents have no place.

Why is this so? Can being stuck in a nuclear arrangement be avoided? What can we do to improve the situation? To help you begin to answer these questions, I want to familiarize you with the nuclear family arrangement. As you read on, you may gain some deeper insight into your own family circumstances as you compare it with what follows.

Stuck in the Nuclear Family

The nuclear family is like an island, because two generations of family members live there in relative isolation. Its baseline credo of "personal independence" and two-generational mind-set serves to disconnect parents and children from outside sources of support. Because of its exclusivity, and the lack of communication with grandparents that results, it leads to acrimony between many parents and grandparents, creates separation and alienation, and inflicts pain and disappointment on everyone, especially the youngsters caught in the cross fire.

Many of us have formed nuclear families without thinking much about it. We just follow what everyone else is doing. Take Rick, thirty-eight, father of three youngsters less than five years of age, for example. Like most of us, Rick experiences constant and unrelenting pressure to fulfill a broad variety of responsibilities. He is obligated to nurture and care for his children, to maintain a household, to meet work demands, to fulfill his personal needs, and to maintain a variety of relationships. Describing his life, he says he feels "drawn and quartered between work and family, being selfish and selfless, between son-hood, husband-hood, fatherhood, and more." Rick shares the daily care of his children with his wife, Jan, thirty-five.

Rick is not happy with his life. Mired in what he feels to be an untenable situation, he is searching for a new way to balance his family responsibilities, work, play, and personal time. "I moved away from my parents to get a good job," Rick told me. "That's what all of my peers did—automatically. I thought Jan and I could do it all. I never, never, ever thought about what it would be like raising three children by ourselves. I can't afford outside help. As an accountant, I can't put in the hours I need to because I care for the kids while Jan works. So my career is suffering. Also I don't want my kids raised by strangers in a day-care center, and that will happen if I go to work full-time. There's gotta be a better way, and I want to find it. This nuclear family deal that me and my friends are living with is for the birds. Too much fallout."

When I asked Rick if his own parents were able to help, he answered, "They are retired in Florida, eight hundred miles away. What can they do?" I asked him if he ever considered asking them to move back near him.

"I can't ask them. They are too old."

"Did you ask them if they thought they were too old to help?"

"Never entered my mind," he answered. "They've got their own lives."

Rick is typical of many of us today. We bought the nuclear family idea. That's why we ended up being geographically and psychologically (or both) autonomous and independent from, as opposed to enmeshed with, our family of origin. And that's why so many of us have become two-dimensional parents.

The Decline of Two-Dimensional Parenthood

Parents in nuclear families are limited to functioning in two dimensions—parent and child. This is a narrow and imploded arrangement unsuited to meet many of its members' needs. Historically, families have always operated in a multidimensional way, including a broad variety of family members, some blood related and some not. It is only recently that the nuclear family appeared in the industrialized world. Its intellectual underpinnings are based on ideas about an individual's *emotional independence*, and *autonomy* from the family of origin.

These notions appeared in the early 1900s and were promulgated by psychoanalysis. This philosophy (revolutionary at the time) soon spread to most first-world nations (but nowhere as strongly as in the United States). As psychoanalysis and psychology expanded, a portion of the movement became corrupted and generated a culture of *narcissism* (self-centeredness) that developed its own language (enmeshment versus autonomy, independence versus dependency and commitment). People became obsessed with self. National movements dedicated to "self-realization" spawned the *me generation*. You know the rest.

Fortunately, like so many ideas and movements, the nuclear family idea is running out of steam. In my opinion, it just does not work. Many of us who were brought up in this era, like Rick, are beginning to recognize the emotional, social, and spiritual costs of two-dimensional family living. We are feeling its harmful and isolating effects on our children as well. Like Rick, we no longer want to perpetuate this system into another generation.

What's Wrong with the New Social Contract

"You grow up, become independent, move away from your family, and start your own" refers to a road map for living that I identified in the late 1970s as the *new social contract*.[2] It came into being in the last century. Consciously or not, most of us are parties to this contract too.

This family contract designated the principles of emotional or personal independence, autonomy, and no enmeshment with one's family of origin. As a result, many of us lead disconnected lives. This is exaggerated by increased geographical mobility and economic opportunity (moving to where the jobs are for the young and moving to the sun belt for retired seniors). When children come along, and support is needed, we find ourselves independent, autonomous, for sure, but also alone, overburdened, and disconnected.

In the nuclear family arrangement, the family roster is restricted to two generations—mom, dad, and the kids. Another tenet of this contract pronounces that the friends and peers of our generation will become our advisers and teachers, to the exclusion of elders. Counseling by peers, media, and paid strangers (professionals) replaces elders as the source of wisdom and experience.

In fact, elders are urged to move to the fringes of society. We placate them, kindly and innocuously dub them "seniors," and relegate them to spending their "golden years" with their own peer group, sharing special interests, far out of the way— emotionally and geographically. As a result, we indeed have structured our society like a *social parfait*—layers of generational separation and stratification according to age groups—each generation in its own stratum. The problem is that the borders between the layers are often ironclad, allowing no blending at all. We have given each layer a name too— "boomers," "gen-Xers," "yuppies," and more.

This social parfait is greatly exploited by business interests who see veins of gold between these layers. One especially unfortunate result is the birth of a powerful teenage culture with plenty of spending money (from who knows where). This *cohort,* as social scientists term it, is seemingly accountable only to itself, supported by marketing and media, and vulnerable to exploitation by sometimes reprehensible business people. Saddest of all, this group of children, without a close personal relationship with an elder, has been essentially cut off from the great benefits of wisdom and experience that are there for the asking.

Grandparents have had mixed feelings about this new social contract. Some have felt "amputated" from their families. Others have been happy to get away to retire and relax. Some have just taken off. Take, for example, one newly self-liberated, feminist grandmother in the 1970s, who jettisoned her motherhood (and grandmotherhood) along with the bathwater of what she referred to as her "life under male oppression."

"I raised my kids and that's it. It's what *I* want from now on," she announced on her way to work for the first time in her life, at age fifty-five. She left a bewildered daughter in her wake (lamenting the loss of her previously "always available" mother) as well as an eight-year-old grandson who called himself a "grandorphan." It wasn't only feminist grandmothers, however, who signed the new social contract. Indeed grandparents of both genders, recently imbued with unexpected and newfound longevity and affluence, have ended their close family involvement and have moved away to retire, work, or travel, leaving more grandorphans in the lurch.

This new social contract was in full swing when I started medical practice in 1960. Since then, the idea of the nuclear family and the generationally stratified society it has created now supplies the mainstream model in our nation. Of course, there are exceptions to the rule. A diversity of first- and second-generation immigrant families and some ethnic minorities (Native Americans, for example), some of whom have been in the United States for centuries, still operate in a multigenerational mode but may not function in harmony as a family team.

Having an extended family system is not an advantage if it is not a healthy and vibrant one. During my work in many of these cultures, I found out that many of these close family systems can be rife with "inherited" conflicts and problems that are passed on from generation to generation. On the one hand, their multigenerational structure is wonderful in that it offers a lot of support for parents, and for grandparents, who regularly care for children. On the other hand, it can be destructive in that it perpetuates the same problems from one generation to the next.

Parents can become easily disillusioned and disheartened in the two-dimensional nuclear family. These effects are experienced *intrapsychically*—that is, within the individual's awareness, identity, values, sense of life meaning, and personal choices. Rick professes unhappiness with the status quo and with the prospect of a similar future for his children. He realizes that it is too hard to keep things going effectively without being too exhausted, feeling frustrated and discontented, and missing his children's childhood. Some single parents also tell me that it is impossible to do anything right (as they would like to), and they are unhappy with the compromises they have to make. What is your situation like?

Change Is on the Way

The good news is that many of us today are trying to reach out beyond the boundaries of the nuclear system. Those of us who depend on paid strangers or child-care institutions to care for our children are reexamining such choices. We are beginning to weigh the *financial rewards* against the *emotional price* we are paying, and many are deciding that the emotional and spiritual cost is too high. As Livia, a twenty-nine-year-old mother with a two-month-old baby, told me, "How do I breast-feed my child if I have to work? Pumping my breasts, storing the milk, and having a baby-sitter give him my milk in a bottle doesn't cut it for me. So I will have to stop."

But Livia didn't have to stop work completely. That's because she asked her parents for help. They pitched in financially so she could work part-time (she is a police dispatcher) for a while. On her workdays, her parents brought her baby to her (weather permitting) for morning feedings. Like Livia, increasing numbers of parents are sharing child care and are recruiting grandparents to participate. Because we are beginning to realize that grandparents can offer solutions to some of our problems, we are seeking to solidify our relationships. This extends beyond child care to educational, social, and financial obligations and responsibilities.

More good news is that our changing attitudes are being mirrored by many of today's new, long-living, and vital grandparents. They want "out" of the new social contract too. The "high" that many grandmothers felt because of women's liberation (especially those who relinquished a very involved grandmotherhood by choosing to enter the work world out of choice rather than necessity), has receded. Like Betty Friedan, they have discovered the joys of grandmotherhood that she describes so well in her book *The Fountain of Age*.

That's not all. Many grandparents who left their families to retire to sunnier climes have begun to reassess their priorities and are seeking a more balanced life. They are beginning to realize how hard it is for parents today (especially single parents). Furthermore they see the effects of parent stress on their grandchildren. As they realize that the philosophy that asserts "I raised my kids and that's it" is wrong, and the philosophy that asserts "parenting is forever" is correct, they want to help.

Do you see these forces at play in your own family? As a reflection of these changing ways, over eight million grandparents are now directly helping and raising their grandchildren when parents falter. Tens of millions more are involved in caring for their grandchild on a part-time basis to supplement parents' efforts. As this phenomenon continues to grow, the reality of increased longevity means that millions of people will be grandparents for more than one-half of their lives, and they will want to know how to live this role to the fullest. We can take advantage of this mounting interest of grandparents to help find a way to be an effective parent and grandparent by recruiting them for our family team.

This shift in parents' and grandparents' attitudes means that receptivity for the idea of building a family team is on the increase. Our first steps in this direction are to overcome the emotional baggage of the past, rekindle the family flames, strengthen attachments, and get to work to create the family team. So instead of moving away to retire, some grandparents are now moving to where their children live. Actually, I know one set of grandparents who did this five times. Some others are returning from retirement to help their children and grandchildren in acute or chronic emergencies.

Increasing numbers of grandparents are making a point to be close by when new grandchildren are born. Some, at the parent's invitation, are observing the birth right when it happens in the delivery room. Young marrieds are starting to consider the option of settling down near grandparents when they decide to start their own families. This was inconceivable twenty years ago. At that time, many people automatically went where the jobs were or made it a point to move away from their families. In the words of a young mother who admits she made a mistake by moving as "far away as possible" from her parents, "I wanted more than anything to be on my own. After my first child, I knew it was the dumbest thing I ever did. Here I had a mother of my own who raised six kids, and I had to call the emergency room for advice every time my baby threw up."

The Next Step

Summing up, the nuclear family has no cohesiveness, no center, and no personality. Elders have no significant role in family life. In the nuclear model, there is no past, present, or future, no master plan. In this family arrangement, altruism, kindness, and interest in one another's welfare are viewed as "intrusive," "controlling," "stifling," and "meddling." The generations can easily be at odds with one another. All of these factors are exactly the opposite of what characterizes the three-dimensional family.

We're now ready to create our own three-dimensional family. But first, you have to know exactly what a three-dimensional family looks like and how it works. In the following chapter, I will show you an ideal family structure that you can use as a working model to enhance your present circumstances.

2

Sticking Together: The Family Team

> Yeah, I have a big family. From my great-grandpa, who is
> ninety-two, to my little brother, who is ten months old. And we
> all stick together.
>
> —Anne-Marie, eleven years old

Now that you are familiar with the limitations of the nuclear family arrangement, let's consider another family arrangement. This family structure is natural, as it is biologically based. Its effectiveness is supported by history, experience, and research. As I hope I have shown, it is the family system that children want and need—the family plan with something for everybody. I call this the *three-dimensional family team*.

The family team that I will describe is no longer standard issue for the majority of our society. Nevertheless most of us have what is necessary to put it together. Certainly, we can start with a nuclear family as its core and assemble it piece by piece, using the family members we have at hand. Once assembled, this new configuration needs constant fine-tuning to keep it running smoothly. For example, we will encounter family members with quirks and foibles, who will, purposely or not, try to gum up the works. (Not to worry. In a later chapter, I will show you how to deal effectively with such folks.) Even when everyone has the will to work in harmony, the foibles of human nature (conflicting attitudes, personalities, and more) will also gum up the works from time to time. Fortunately, most of these glitches can be easily repaired. As I proceed to describe the characteristics of this ideal family situation, keep the reality of your present family situation in mind.

Characteristics of the Family Team

What follows is based on the studies that I mentioned in the Introduction. As I also mentioned, I've come to believe that the three-dimensional family team is the best human system in which to grow and manage a family. It offers us the optimum soil for each of us to grow into a three-dimensional parent. And because it contains grandparents, it's perfectly suited for us to access grandparent solutions when needed.

Briefly put, the family team is composed of blood-related people, who are rooted in the past, live in the present, and plan for the future. The family team is built around an interwoven child-parent-grandparent center. It's much like a *triple helix*—three independent strands, intertwined. With the strands of other family members added to this core, the family can be exponentially strengthened. For the purposes of this book, however, I will limit myself to addressing the core child-parent-grandparent component and refer to it as the family team per se.

Many of the family members that I originally interviewed for this study live within a one-hour drive of one another. Others live many miles apart. Although their proximity to one another may be different, their engagement and membership on the family team can be quite similar (as I will explain later). I've learned that whether they're distanced or not, family members can be a team in spirit. I should also mention that a number of families in my study worked together, either in farming or in a family business.

Please bear with me if you think my description of people who live according to this model and philosophy seems overly sentimental and idealized. As schmaltzy as it may sound, these descriptions nevertheless reflect a true picture of their lives. The reason for all the emotion is that the family team is based on an affectionate emotional attachment, as well as a spiritual philosophy. For some, it may be difficult to read what follows without becoming skeptical, sad, envious, irritated, or even incredulous.

"Do such families really exist?" one person asked me.

They do. Yet nothing is perfect. These folks have as many foibles, feuds, and eccentricities as anyone else. What is most impressive about them, however, is their ability to maintain close emotional bonds and family unity even under the most adverse circumstances. The family team sticks together. Here are a few of the general characteristics of the people who live as family team members.

Parents on the Family Team

Parents who are fortunate enough to be members of a family team seem to have achieved a level of emotional maturity that is manifested in the *readiness* for parenthood. These individuals have devoted sufficient time to learning about themselves, sowing their wild oats, and fulfilling some of their personal dreams and goals before devoting their life to a child. Before they even considered parenthood, they spent time becoming familiar with their partner.

The great majority are formally married, as opposed to just living together. They are aware of the costs of parenthood and are ready to pay the price. Couples know that becoming parents alters the impulsive and carefree aspect of their independence. It also alters their mutual relationship and diminishes the undivided one-to-one attention they can give to each other.

They share their joy about impending parenthood with their family, and especially (each) with their own parents. The impending birth often becomes a family affair, and family members pitch in to help—especially grandparents. Parents are ready to be at the central command post of a three-dimensional family team. The readiness factor is very important.

Having a child within the context of a family team makes relationships, marriage, and parenthood run smoother. Whenever the pressures of parenthood overwhelm one parent or another, the supportive family, and especially grandparents, easily absorbs any spillover.

"It's so helpful to us, my husband and me, to have my parents so happy when we go off. They just can't wait to have our kids," Muriel, thirty-three, told me. The family team supplies enough supportive people so that parents have a great deal of support and do not have the pressure to be all things to one another.

Earl, thirty-six, said, "I am so glad that Alice, my wife, has her mother and sisters to talk to. There's stuff that I can't help her with. She needs her family. I can't be her mother, sister, and girlfriend too. Sure I am her best friend, but married people aren't supposed to supply it all for one another; it isn't human. For example, Alice doesn't like to fish, and I do. With her family around, we're all happier. She yaks with her sisters. I go fishin'."

Children on the Family Team

Children raised among a family team feel that they are in an *emotional paradise*. They sense that they are important because they *are* important to and cherished by family members. They feel deeply secure as well, because they have their parents and grandparents who love them and are available to them when things get rough. Being so connected to others, children (temperament aside) usually are friendly, like and respect people, and are socially adept. Many like to use titles when addressing elders, such as "grandma," for example, and endearing terms too, such as "auntie" or "nana."

They respect their elders, as Tilly, ten, demonstrates. "My grandmother is old; look at all the family she has. Can you imagine all she did to bring all these people along? She is so cute and everyone is crazy about her. I want to be like her. She raised eight children and ran a grocery store. Wonder Woman, that's my grandmother."

With a large, loving, and supportive family, youngsters learn an optimistic view of family life and look forward to continuing their own family someday. One important finding is that in a larger family environment, childhood is prolonged—kids are allowed to remain kids—and no one is in a hurry for them to grow up. And they feel *useful* too, a rarity for children today. This is especially true for those children in rural areas, who often contribute relevantly to their family (chores, gardening, animal care, and so forth). Even deeper, they know that their existence brings family members joy!

Children in family teams are usually listened to and can influence adults, whether it is making their loved ones happy by just being themselves, or being together with adults, or doing helpful chores or jobs. There are few latchkey kids in this group. It seems that someone is always available for them. They care for one another too, with many children of twelve and above caring for their juniors. All are close to their grandparents, and parents are active in fostering the relationship.

Although their love and attachment is constant, it is manifested differently at different ages. Young children have few bones to pick. One of the most telling signs of a family's health is the way it copes with adolescents. In this group, some adolescents (who can find fault even in paradise) complain that the closeness and caring of the family team is "stifling." Others find that following family tradition is something to rebel against. As Erin, twelve, said, "My family is uncool, but I love them." The good part is that adolescents in conflict with parents also have access to grandparents and other family members when they need it.

As Evelyn, forty-two, said, "Having a large family is a blessing. My daughter, Katie, is sixteen and feeling her oats. She drives me nuts. Whenever I sit on her, she gets mad and stomps out. But I know she goes no further than my parents' or my sister's house to complain about me."

Grandparents and Great-Grandparents on the Family Team

The family team is the channel through which elders share the wisdom and experience that they have accumulated through the years. Just as they did in more primitive times, grandparents serve as the family team's wise and experienced role models that parents often look up to for example and to define the philosophy by which they live. The older the person, the more respect he or she has in the family, and especially if the elder is sprightly and communicative. As an entitlement, elders are given an important ceremonial role in family functions and celebrations.

A young man told me that his ninety-six year-old great-grandfather "stands as the head of the family. He doesn't do much, but he doesn't have to. All he has to do is to be there." I will explain why this young man feels this way in the next chapter. The status of elders on the family team is markedly different from the status of those elders who are isolated and alienated—and even useless—in our ageist society today.

The Local Life of the Family Team

The members of the family team are involved with one another in a very specific and important local life. They spend social time with one another, gather at family celebrations or holidays, even work together. Child care is shared by all generations as much as possible. That is why children feel so secure. Family members have well-defined roles that shift back and change according to age, need, and ability. They function independently but in continuity. As a result, they rarely invade one another's territory without invitation. Boundaries are clear. A grandmother, for example, may take over a parenting role in the parents' absence when requested, but she will back off and return to being a supportive grandmother when the parents return.

Family members communicate directly and are open with their feelings. Each family member's self-image is strongly dependent on family standing, no matter the degree of material wealth or social status.

The best example I know of is John, a blacksmith I met in a small New England town in 1981. John is highly respected by his family.

His mother describes him affectionately: "I have a son who makes a lot of money in New York, but frankly, he is not half the son that John is."

For John, his family is his "reason for living." "I know I don't make such a good living, but I make enough to keep going. Anyway there are things that count more. I am loved, needed, and important in my family. The people that I care about love me—that's what counts for me. I am not interested in moving away for an important job, or more money. Life is local for me."

Members of this kind of family team make it a point to respect the differences and the individuality of its members' temperament, character, interests, and talents. The fact that they relate according to their biological relationship—parent, grandparent, uncle, and so forth—offers a sense of place and order.

Ned, nine years old, described this pecking order: "Uncle John can't boss me around like my father or mother can. He can take me places and give me ideas, but he can't punish me. He hasn't the right like my parents or grandparents have. And sometimes my grandparents can tell my parents what to do . . . but they talk with them nice."

How the Family Team Copes with Hard Times

When hardship strikes, the family is mobilized. When the challenge comes from outside the family, they band together. Jack, forty-three, lost his small neighborhood diner when the World Trade Center was destroyed on September 11, 2001. His business was next door to the twin towers, so he narrowly escaped with his life when the buildings collapsed next to his store and debris flooded in through his windows. He lost everything—furniture, equipment, and inventory—and remained shocked and devastated for many months afterward. After he began to recover from the trauma, he and his wife sat down to hammer out a plan for a comeback. Soon the rubble would be cleared to a point where he could have access to rebuild his diner.

Jack and his wife are very close to his parents. Together they constitute a strong family team. It was therefore natural for Jack to include his parents in his plan. Before he could ask, they said that they would mortgage their house to help Jack raise the necessary capital to start anew. The family team came to the rescue.

Serious but Never Fatal Conflicts in the Family Team

When challenges arise within a family team—for example, personality clashes or personal feuds—the sparks often fly. No matter how intense the dispute, however, the family usually makes it through without grudges or estrangement.

Unlike the members of more tenuous family arrangements, family team members who are feuding try not to cut off from one another emotionally. If they cannot reconcile by themselves, there are always others—family peacemakers and arbiters—who urge them to heal the conflict.

Nana, eighty-three, a California grandmother, says, "I have twelve grandchildren and six kids and one or another of them are constantly at one another. This husband hates this brother-in-law. It goes on and on. I get in there and straighten it all out. They really don't mind me butting in, either. Sometimes they back themselves into a corner with their big mouths. Someone has got to bail them out. It all comes out in the wash. Our family is important to everyone, so they know that problems have to be solved. Sooner is better than later. The kids don't like it when there is trouble." When problems that are more serious occur, family members usually exhaust their personal resources before turning to social institutions or "paid strangers" for help.

Family Ego and Tradition

The family culture should be respected by its members. Many of the families that I've known express a sense of pride in their families and talk about a *family ego*.

"I am an O'Rourke," said eleven-year-old Siobhan. "We O'Rourkes are good at dancing and art. Being an O'Rourke means I have to act a certain way or else I could shame my family. I am not saying it is easy, or I like it, but I do it. I love my family and will always help anyone who needs me."

Elders are important for sustaining the family culture and pride. They teach by example and demonstrate the value of this family philosophy. Family ways are handed down by tradition. "We do the same things over and over for every generation," said Mary Belle, seventy-two. "Same church, same holidays. I am in charge of keeping it all straight. Like my grandmother did." Like Mary Belle's family, other family teams also have an emotional or spiritual leader. The leader is usually designated in an unspoken decision.

Take, for example, Jason, eighty-nine, a farmer in Appalachia, who is an ideal grandfather and the leader of his family. He has identified the person who will one day assume his duty to "watch out for the family." One afternoon, as we were standing on the front porch of his farm on a hot summer's day, looking out over his fields, his young granddaughter Sarah was cavorting on the grass in front of us with her new puppy. "She's next when her mother passes on," said Jason. "She'll be the heart of our family, just like her mother, just like her grandmother and Elsa, her great-grandmother. She's got what it takes."

Their main unifying forces are the family personality (family members speak of themselves as "we"), being geographically near to one another (a critical factor), and spending time with one another. These factors—time, place, and undivided attention to one another—are the basic ingredients of the vital connection. Together these factors create deep emotional attachments between people. With vital connections, emotional bonds are not viewed as emotional bondage. Adversity is more easily absorbed. New additions to the family, by adoption or remarriage, and family friends can be included and accepted as "kin" automatically.

The Family Team Credo

The ideal family team system works because of an unspoken contract between its members that can be stated as a *credo*:

- The family is a multidimensional entity.
- Family members are multigenerational.
- Family members will be committed to and support one another.

- Family members share a common philosophy and values.
- Family members love and cherish their children.
- Family members will honor and tolerate their differences.
- Family members will recognize and resolve their conflicts.
- Family members stay in the family.
- Family members will openly communicate with one another about the state of their family.
- Newcomers are welcomed.

Now that you are acquainted with the "ideal" characteristics of the family team, compare them with the characteristics of your own family. Every similarity is an asset. The core of the family team is the child-parent-grandparent relationship.

Now it is time to begin to assess your family, address any outstanding issues, and enhance the relationship between you, your parents, and your children. To begin, you need to learn something about the complex workings of these relationships. This is the subject of the next chapter.

3

Members of the Family Team: You, Your Child, and Your Parents

When my parents get on my case, I go to my grandparents' house. They tell me the same thing as my parents, but they are not as mad.

—Silvano, sixteen years old

The emotional glue that binds together the three-dimensional family team is the love and ability to live in harmony. Our ability to live in harmony depends on our personality type, age, attitudes, experiences, health, fortune, and life circumstances.

Observe how our own parents have changed with age. Age has its benefits for parents as well. My research has shown that grandparents rarely repeat the mistakes that they made as parents with their grandchildren. This is good news because it means that there is a good chance that no matter what "miseries" our parents inflicted on us as we grew up (unless we are talking about blatant pathology), they won't repeat the same mistakes with our child. Nature gives grandparents another chance. So should we.

Playing the Appropriate Role

Each person on the family team has a specific and unique role to play. For example, in spite of some exceptions to the rule, my research shows that like parents, grandfathers and grandmothers play out their roles differently. Consequently, we want to be careful of what we expect and ask from each of them.

For example, most grandmothers are very involved and interested in babies. As Lillian, a seventy-five-year-old grandmother, said, "I wouldn't let a grandfather loose with any baby before it can walk. They treat it like a football." Generally speaking, grandfathers are good for emergencies of a physical and financial nature, manual labor, stories, dealing with sickness, adventures, taking kids for lessons, making stuff, breaking the rules, stating the value of manners and education, grandfatherly type discipline, and being good role models.

Grandmothers are good for emergencies of a personal and emotional nature, worrying, dealing with bodily functions, babies, changing diapers, feeding, burping, clothes, more worrying, manners, dealing with sickness, potty training, food, fun, and being good role models. From personal and professional experience, I can testify that grandfathers aren't always good for buying baby clothes, or for detecting when a child has to use the potty. The point of all this is that when you call on grandparents for help, remember the "central-casting" idea. You might first ask grandpa to start your car on a freezing morning or grandma to go shopping with you for baby and kiddie clothes. Use grandparents for what they do well, according to the age of your child. These role differentiations that I currently find in my research will blur in the future. That's because today's more nurturing fathers will become grandfathers, and today's mothers, who are working out feverishly and running marathons and becoming more physically strong and skilled, will become grandmothers.

This said, each member of your family team has an individual role and unique relationships. As a parent, we already know all about the parent-child bond, so let's now consider the intricacies of what takes place between the people on the other two ends of your family team. You can use this information to better understand what is taking place in your own family, and for future reference.

Grandparents and Your Child

Grandparents offer your child love, adoration, safety, security, learning, and fun. They are a natural extension of you as a GRANDparent—the parent's parent. The closer our child is to a grandparent, the better it is for us. My research shows that children with close grandparents feel deeply attached to and identified with loving adults, families, and communities. They feel emotionally secure because *they matter*, they feel precious, and they know that they are important to adults. Andy, ten, said, "I am my grandmother's precious jewel. She calls me that all the time."

Grandparents offer children who are having problems with parents a safe emotional retreat. Here, with a parent's blessing, they can receive comfort, an attentive ear, and advice in a safe place. This is a win-win situation because parents can feel secure that their children are in safe hands. We shouldn't be surprised if our child asks grandparents (as *our* own parents, thus a "higher authority") to intercede with us.

Children benefit greatly from the variety of their grandparents' experience. Through grandparents, children are exposed to other languages, values, cultures, and ways of thinking. By learning through their grandparents' stories and examples, children can think "out of the box," because they are not dependent only on their own learning or experience to understand the world. They have the opportunity to learn history firsthand from relatives who lived the events: from their parents about events in the recent past, from their grandparents about events in the distant past, and from their great-grandparents about events from long, long ago. Children absorb our parents' attitudes, skills, religious convictions, and parenting styles. They carefully observe how we interact with their grandparents. An added bonus for a child is that a close grandparent relationship develops a positive attitude toward older people, and to our child's future old age.

The Genetic Connection

As you will learn when you become a grandparent in your own right, the urge to grandparent is a deeply rooted emotional and behavioral instinct similar to parenting, just notched up one generation. Like parents and children, grandparents and grandchildren are related genetically. As parents, we are genetically connected to both generations. Just as we carry one-half of each of our parent's genes, our child carries one-quarter of them. Therefore *our parents are in our child.* That's why our child can resemble our parents physically and may inherit their (ideally good) attitudes, talents, temperaments, and even their foibles. Genes are destiny, and there's not too much anyone can do about it. This can be very evident in some cases.

I have met some parents who were hard put to relate to their own child because the child bore such a close resemblance to a parent they disliked.

Wim, twelve, said, "My mother is always mad at me. She says I have the bad habits of her father, my grandfather, who was mean to her. He is dead now. I never met him. She always looks at me angry as if I did something wrong. I try to be good but I can't please her."

His mother, Mira, thirty-eight, was aware of her behavior. "I know I am wrong, but when I look at Wim, I see my father. It's like he is haunting me."

This works in a positive way too, as when a child is seen as a "chip off the old block," and the "block" is loved and cherished. "Yeah," smiled Ethel, fifteen, "everyone tells me I am just like grandma. She was one of the first women doctors in the country, and I am going to be one too."

The grandchild-grandparent duo is "hardwired" to be with each other and to transmit wonderful things back and forth. Our child transfers love and joy; our parents transfer the benefit of their roles, as well as being unconditionally in love with our child. Grandparent love is different from our parental love, which necessarily has an instructional, conditional quality attached. We have to supervise and monitor children's behavior and act as the family teacher and "police force." Not so for grandparents. They get a better deal (although they paid their dues as parents).

As with parenthood, the emotional aspects of grandparenthood start even before the first child comes along and ripen with age as the grandparent hones the skills of nonreactivity, nonjudgment, compassion, and tolerance. During my research, I have identified a built-in drive to grandparent, similar to the drive most of us feel when we want to become a parent. The drive makes itself known, at a specific readiness time, even before a grandchild comes along. At this juncture, the future grandparent begins to experience thoughts, feelings, and behavior—an urge—related to having a grandchild. Without a grandchild, some report yearnings to be a grand-parent. (This can be annoying to an adult child who is not ready—or so inclined—to have a baby.)

When a grandchild is born, even geographically distant grand-parents report this powerful urge to be with their grandchild. An example is Roger, sixty-five, a long-distance grandfather, who reported what he experienced when his son called him to tell him he was a grandfather: "I want desperately to see my first grandchild, to feel her close to me, to hear her voice, to count her fingers and toes."

Grandparents report the urge to bond emotionally with the child as soon as it is born. They feel a need to imprint the child in their mind and to support the parents. This can be an especially close moment for mothers and daughters. It is at this time that many parents report the love and pride that they feel about giving their own parents the gift of a grandchild. That's why it is important for us to include grandparents in the prenatal and birth process whenever possible.

Overall the grandparenting drive that our parents experience is expressed and fulfilled by the *new roles* that they play for our child. Fulfilling these roles contributes to their positive self-concept of being a grandparent and to their confidence that we and our child will eventually value what they do.

Special Roles of the Grandparent

These natural grandparent roles supply our parent with a twofold job description. The first is how to grandparent our child. The sec-ond is how to parent us as adults. When grandparents understand these different roles and fulfill them in different ways, and at differ-ent times, according to the family's needs, I call them "effective grandparents." Simply put, grandparents are doing what nature has prescribed for them to do. Effective grandparents supply us and our child with a blueprint for our own grandparenting in the future. Among the most important roles that I have identified to date are the following:

Ancestor

Buddy

Hero

Historian

Mentor

Nurturer

Spiritual guide

Student

Teacher

Wizard

Each role is unique. Roles such as mentor, nurturer, teacher, and student are practical and informative. The ancestor and historian roles offer an added dimension of emotional wonder and connectivity for our child, drawn from the unseen past. Grandparents' magical roles, such as hero, spiritual guide, and wizard, are packed full of emotional, psychological, sentimental, and spiritual qualities that are sometimes beyond the ability of parents to discern, unless they experienced their benefits as grandchildren.

Because both our child and our parents grow and change over the years, nature has fine-tuned these roles to be dynamic and responsive. (That's why we well may find our father more laid-back as a grandfather than he was as a young father.)

Very often, grandparents make up for what they couldn't do as parents. They may have been too busy struggling to support their family; they may have been less selfless and mature. There could have been a lot of reasons for this. But people learn from and

and their mistakes. So as the years pass, grandparents may play different roles, in different degrees of intensity, for our child. For example, the roles of ancestor, historian, and hero remain consistent. In contrast, grandparents play more of a physical nurturing role for a very young child and more of an emotional nurturing role as the child matures. The mentoring role becomes more important as the child grows older.

Grandparents' behaviors serve consistently as a role model for parents and children. Changing family needs affect these roles. For example, if our child gets enmeshed in the middle of a family crisis, we might call on grandparents to help. And of course, there is always baby-sitting in the early years. Because it is so important that we know the intricacies of each role, I will explain each briefly. As you read on, keep in mind that you will enact these roles in the future. In addition, relate them to the kind of grandparenting that you see going on at the moment and what you experienced as a youngster.

1. *Ancestor.* As real live ancestors, grandparents represent a more ancient link in our child's ancestral chain. Just as we represent our child's recent historical origins, and just as we embody all that has come before our child, our own parents embody all that has come before us. They fulfill this ancestral role for our child by *just existing.*

   Grandparents contain a storehouse of information about other times and other places: how the family has lived and functioned in the past and how it has survived hard times. This information is transmitted through stories, for which children have genetically built-in receptors. That is because before the written word, grandparents were the repository of knowledge and information on which the society relied. Thus grandparents serve as the reporter of our own living history—our own childhood—for our child.

   Children know instinctively that grandparents know the "real truth" about their parents' childhood. This ancestral connection enforces generational continuity. My research shows that in the young child's mind the oldest grandparent is afforded a special place and great respect. The ancestral role teaches our child, no matter how old she is, that she came from us and that we came from her grandparents, and so on, beyond where memory keeps watch. That is the essence of belonging.

2. *Buddy*. One of the trickiest roles that we have to deal with as a parent is often the most enjoyable and sentimental role for grandparents. That is when they act like a buddy to our child. Here the grandparent can be the light-hearted conspirator, while we play the heavy. It's not much fun for us who have to play the heavy, but it's great fun for children.

Grandparents have a license to be carefree because they are not responsible for the day-to-day tasks involved in running our family. Ideally, you remember some fun with your own grandparent buddy. What goes around comes around. As parents, we do the work, they get the reward.

I do want to alert you to two potential dangers related to this role. The first is that we may well think a grandparent is spoiling our child when the two of them are just having one heck of a good time. A bit of parental envy is normal. If you feel rumblings like this, not to worry. You will get even when you are a grandparent. Second, parents who are not on good terms with their own parents may resent the fun that grandparents are having with the children, especially in this buddy role. When there are serious problems between parents and grandparents, this buddy role is often the first to be adversely affected. Most parents, however, are happy to see their child and parent run off and have a good time together. Actually, if we are smart, *we* should do the same when our child and our parent are so happily occupied.

3. *Hero*. Young children view "old" grandparents differently from the way they see us. "My grandfather is really old," said Eason, fourteen. "He has big wrinkles and he is bowlegged. He was a cowboy." Actually, Eason's grandfather is fifty-five years old,

runs marathons, and can do fifty one-hand push-ups. Wrinkles are badges of courage to youngsters, because each has a story to tell.

Although adults may see a grandparent as old and decrepit, grandchildren see physical durability and emotional strength: perseverance, endurance, and survival. Children need heroes, and these are the qualities of heroes. Although we as parents may be "local heroes" for our child, grandparents are more distant and mysterious. That's because they have lived long and have had adventures in far-off places. Children delight when grandparents relate wild stories and gild the lily a bit.

Take, for example, ten-year-old Ralph's grandfather, who explained his blue-tinted skin: "It was in a cobalt mine in Colorado that my skin turned blue one day. I worked there for five years. One day, I came out of the shaft and I was all blue. Everyone looked at me and yelled that I had turned blue. I looked in the mirror and it was true. The cobalt finally got to me."

4. *Historian*. This is an essential role that our parents play for our child. In this role (complementary to the ancestor role), our parent is the living embodiment of generations past and serves as a living witness to the history of his or her own times as well as the chronicler of the living history of the family's forebears. Reaching back beyond our own memory, their memories and photo albums, jitterbugging, old recipes, and family memorabilia make the past come alive, embody the present, and pass on this legacy to us and our child. This grandparent role is equally important if you have a stepchild or an adopted child.

Grandparents come to this role naturally. Throughout human history, they have served as the repositories of wisdom and history as the oldest generation. Children learn wonderful and special stories from their grandparents about how they may have immigrated to the United States or about what it was like to have seen combat in the Second World War, or to have lived through the economic depression, or to have seen Babe Ruth play. This role enables grandparents to time-travel with our child. We shouldn't be envious. Our opportunity to time-travel will come someday.

5. *Mentor*. There is a special magic to the way grandparents teach grandchildren. Most involved grandparents eventually come to realize that it's not only *what* they teach that matters but *how* it is taught. As mentors, grandparents are cheerleaders firing our child's imagination, inspiring her dreams, nurturing her spirit, and encouraging her intellectual growth while giving her a sense of self-worth. The child absorbs the spirit and the essence of the grandparent while they are together.

   The greatest compliment is for children to model themselves after an excellent grandparent. Leah, fifty-four, became an attorney because her grandfather, "who looked like Abraham Lincoln," taught her about "honesty and defending the innocent." Children receive information from grandparents in an unpressured atmosphere of acceptance and unconditional love. Under such circumstances, grandparents can easily pass on their family skills and secrets.

   Hester, sixteen, who lives on Nantucket Island, learned the family chowder recipe from her grandfather. "He's a pretty quiet person. When I asked him how to make the chowder, he gave me the ingredients and asked me to watch him. He never criticized me when I didn't get it right. He would just taste it and say, 'That's not quite it.' It took me two years to get it right. When I thought I had it, I asked him to taste it. He said, 'That's it. The recipe stays in the family. Now your great-grandchildren will enjoy it too. You are the only one in the family that is interested enough to learn it.' That's all he said. But I soon heard he told everyone in town about it. I knew he was proud."

6. *Nurturer*. As nurturers, grandparents use their wisdom and experience to supply a natural safety net for both us and our child. This role is especially important for us when we are secure in the knowledge that our own parents are available to

help when, and if, adversity strikes. Child care, nursing, counseling, caring for the children while we need respite or spend
needed time together with our partner, and providing financial and emotional support are only a few of the ways that
grandparents can nurture their family.

Nurturing begins before the child is born, when expectant
grandparents share the joy and provide love and support to
expectant parents. Although grandparents seem to know
instinctively what grandchildren need in the form of nurturing, it is important that we coordinate their efforts with
our own.

For example, when a new baby is on the way, it is helpful to
discuss their expectations as grandparents over a family dinner
or when they attend a childbirth training class with us. We
need to let them know our hopes and dreams for ourselves and
our child and what we expect of them.

An effective grandparent will nurture our child—their
grandchild—forever: from the moment the child is born
until the moment the grandparent leaves the earth. This role
reaches beyond biological grandchildren to stepgrandchildren
and adopted children too. Children expect this of grandparents and see grandparents as the next logical support system
after us. "My grandparents are the family ER team," said
Virginia, twelve.

That's why children take it well when they are cared for by
grandparents, in sickness and in health. They know their
grandparents love them and "worry" about their health and
well-being. "Yeah," said Tyler, twelve, "My grandmother . . .
she is the worry queen. If I ever sneeze around her, I've had it.
Out comes the Vicks and the same old lecture about taking
care of myself. . . . I guess that's what grandmothers do." When
problems arise, expect that our child may ask us to turn to the
grandparents to help.

"Why put me in after-school care?" said Rosie, eight years old.
"I'll ask grandma to baby-sit me." From a more mysterious

point of view, children view grandparents as having healing qualities. The older the grandparent, the greater the power could be. Poultices, enemas, and smelly liniments aside, the good stuff, like grandma's special chicken soup or special dessert dish, helps a lot.

7. *Spiritual guide*. Grandparents are programmed to care for our child's spirit, especially when we don't have the time to do the job ourselves. This role reaches beyond any religious beliefs that we practice and can have a profound and lasting effect on the ethical-moral dimension of our child's learning. This role is equally important for a stepchild or adopted child.

Spiritual guidance is about love and wonder—the transforming and illuminating feeling that our child has when he looks into a grandparent's adoring eyes. It is about the smiles, the good times, the joy, the warmth, and the sharing—the sense of life's true meaning—in emotional, sentimental terms, in poetry or literature. It's about what is called the *fruits of the spirit*: love, tolerance, compassion, reverence, joy, peace, gentleness, goodness, faith, and kindness. It is about experiencing more of life than what meets the eye.

Although we may cultivate our child's spirit—teaching ethics, morality, and religious values—grandparents' teachings have an added quality, one that is less purposeful as it concerns day-to-day life. It is rooted beyond the every day in wisdom, experience, a long view of life, and an ever-increasing awareness of one's mortality that children understand. That's because children see grandparents as old, and as temporary in their lives.

As Kyra, sixteen years old, said about her eighty-five-year-old grandfather, "My grandpa, he is great. He knows so much. But I know I won't have him forever because he's got one foot on a banana peel and the other in heaven."

8. *Student*. Did you know that our parents are also our students? Parents and children are among their greatest teachers. That's

because grandparenting, like parenting, is a work in progress. It involves lifelong learning. The process begins as a grand-child, proceeds to parenthood, and on to grandparenthood. From our position in the middle of this three-dimensional chain, we are constantly teaching our own parents.

Keeping the grandparents up-to-date with modern develop-ments is one important way. Children are often the first teach-ers of grandparents when it concerns technology. Our children can also keep their grandparents' lives current and vibrant, instructing them, for example, about the latest music, the new way to do math, or the current way to dress. Adolescents can show them what is "cool" and "modern," and what body-piercing, or tattooing, is all about.

9. *Teacher.* As our child's teacher, a grandparent imparts general information and skills (as opposed to their more specific role as mentor or historian). All that they have learned over the years constitutes their curriculum. Many teach acquired skills that our child will learn nowhere else, such as baking, whit-tling, singing, speaking a foreign language, playing chess, gar-dening, knitting, skiing, swimming, diving, braiding hair. This is so important nowadays because children get so little undi-vided attention from other people, have limited exposure in school, and are taught in such a structured and limited way. This brand of knowledge broadens our child's experience and store of knowledge in a unique way.

10. *Wizard.* This is the most enjoyable, freewheeling, and free-spirited role that grandparents play. It is especially evident with young children. This is also a difficult role for us as par-ents to understand because it has to do with the numinous dimensions of inspiration, magic, the unseen, imagination, romance, and wonder—the stuff that adults are often too busy to contemplate.

My favorite story concerning grandparent wizardry concerns Hallie, six years old. She thought her grandma was "magic" the first time she saw her remove her false teeth. It took Ron, five years old, about a year to figure out that pressing his nose did not turn on the windshield wipers in his grandpa's car. That's because every time his grandfather turned the wipers on, he would press the end of Ron's nose first. And there are always magic tricks, pennies coming out of ears, Christmas, Santa Claus, and the tooth fairy.

As wizards, grandparents can provide a playful, imaginative counterpoint to our child's otherwise task-oriented everyday world. Grandparents do not have to be as vigilant as we do in dealing with discipline. They are therefore free to indulge the child's fantasies and playfulness. This powerful role is recognized and appears in most cultures.

For example, in the Tupian tribe of South America, the grandfather is associated with thunder. Among the Yurok Indians, every grandmother has her own song that has the power to drive away evil spirits. Fairy godmothers have special powers too.

Indeed a child might think that her grandfather and the Wizard of Oz have lots in common. Although their "real" power may differ, her grandfather can make the seemingly impossible happen and encourages her to believe that dreams come true. Perhaps you have received the benefit of this role from a grandparent of your own. This role also offers our child respite from an often too-practical world, encouraging wonder, fancy, and letting the imagination soar beyond the borders of rationality.

Here's an example that I like to tell: Nan, a twenty-five-year-old writer, remembers taking walks with her grandfather when she was a little girl. She recalls how he would encourage her to let her imagination soar: "We would make up stories. We saw a hawk in the sky and made up poems about him. I once saw a woodchuck, and grandfather asked me what it would be like to be a woodchuck and for me to make up a story about where the woodchuck lives and about her family. I wrote a story and drew pictures too. Like a regular children's book. He loved it. The next day, he took me to the woodchuck's den and showed me where she really lived and her babies. He told me that my pictures were better and that imagination could be more interesting than reality."

When a grandparent's wizardry and role as a spiritual guide is mixed with the nurturing role, we have the basis for the shaman, healer, sage, *curandera,* or whatever the culture calls the "medicine" person. Children know this instinctively. Science cannot explain why a grandparent's prayers, blessings, and special potions often work. Placebo? Sure. Something extra? Absolutely.

Parents as the Gatekeepers

As parents, we act as a linchpin between our child and our parents. To do our best in this job, we need to make room in our lives to bring them together. This is one of our greatest responsibilities as parents.

Of course, this is no easy task today because we are so busy, and so is our child. Violet, a thirty-four-year-old parent of three, "goes crazy" when her parents come to visit. She says, "My kids are so busy with their activities, lessons, soccer games. Whenever my parents show up, it is rare if more than one of my kids is at home. The kids want to see their grandparents, but there just doesn't seem to be any time because they are so busy."

We serve as the gatekeeper between our child and our parent. So busy or not, this is a primary responsibility that we have to fulfill to the best of our ability. The grandparent roles that I have described are there for our child's taking, when we encourage our own parents to deliver them.

For example, when our child is in need of care, or finances, call on the nurturing role. If academic help after school is necessary, ask a grandparent to help as a teacher, or mentor, with tutoring.

The degree to which we can access grandparent solutions to our problems depends on the quality of our relationship with them. The better the relationship, the stronger our family team and the more we can ask of grandparents.

We begin to activate our family team by accentuating the positive and eliminating any negatives that exist today. We start to accentuate the positive by reaching out to grandparents, having fun with them, and spending time together. To eliminate the negative, we begin by addressing and overcoming any difficulties from the past. We start by addressing and resolving any simmering past conflicts or problems between our parents, our in-laws, and us. This is often not an easy task, but I hope that the advice and guidance you will find in the next chapter will be helpful.

PART TWO

Building the Family Team

4

Overcoming the Past: Guidelines for the Future

There are two kinds of grandparent members on our family team—our parents and our partner's parents, that is, our in-laws. Our deep bond with our own parents is permanent. It reaches back to our beginnings, and whether good or bad, it is always with us. In contrast, our relationship with our partner's parents may run the gamut from being close to distant, loving to adversarial. Single parents may have only their own parents to count on (with some exceptions in the case of close ex-in-laws).

Divorce and remarriage complicate these relationships. To avoid any potential confusion with terms, I will refer to our natural parents, our in-laws, and our ex-in-laws collectively as grandparents. As I mentioned previously, our relationship with them can be a blessing when we get along well. Conversely, it can range from an annoying burden to a pervasive emotional disaster when we have conflicts. In addition, the interactions that we have with grandparents, for better or worse, affect our child, partner, and the rest of the family.

The in-law relationship can be especially complicated. Because these grandparents are our partner's parents, we do not have the same measure of direct control, influence, or history that we do in dealing with our own parents. When our relationship with an in-law is going well, all the better. If the converse is true, then we can have triple trouble. When we do not get along with our in-laws, our child's relationship with them can be adversely affected, as well as our relationship with our partner. And this is even more so when we disagree with our partner about the cause or nature of the conflict.

There is no worse situation than to be caught in the middle of a feud between our own parent and our spouse or between our spouse and our spouse's parent. This typically happens with the well-known "mother-in-law syndrome." In this situation, one partner has to deal with the other's critical or overly possessive (of their own child) parent. Jokes aside, it is not very funny when this condition ends up causing a serious rift in an otherwise happy relationship. When aggravated by stressful circumstances, such as divorce or remarriage, any previously contentious situation can easily spin out of control.

Coping with Normal Conflicts

Most of us will encounter day-to-day conflicts and problems with grandparents. When they do occur, we need to limit their effect so that our adult conflicts don't taint the grandparent-grandchild relationship. We must be extra vigilant to spare children the emotional fireworks that accompany adult conflicts. Children are acutely aware of what is happening around them and intently observe how adults handle adversity. That is why it is so important for us to deal with conflict competently.

I cannot emphasize this too strongly. No matter how negative we may feel about another person at a given time, *if only for our child's sake*, it is important that we strive as best we can to resolve any differences. That example is the best we can do for our child. Our efforts will pay off in the future, when we inevitably will go head-to-head with our child over our future differences.

The battles we have with grandparents are fought on the field of our present and historical relationship with them. Where there is love and commitment, conflicts are regarded as the cost of doing family business and are quickly resolved. All should be more easily forgiven.

Past relationships are especially important. This is usually not so much of a problem with in-law grandparents, because there is usually only a brief common historical past and personal history. The relationship is more present oriented, so it is devoid of past emotional baggage. That is why wonderful in-laws can be easily promoted to first-stringers on our family team. With biological parents, however, the past is extensive and may be fraught with pain and suffering. This needs to be put right. That is why it is so important, as we proceed to build our first-string family team, to address and resolve any past difficulties with our own parents and start anew.

Overcoming the Past

It's crucial for the success of our family team that we unload any emotional baggage—thoughts, feelings, memories, anger, resentment, grudges, and more—that we have accumulated while growing up with our own parents. If we cannot make the effort to forgive and forget (significant pathology as the exception), we cannot build a strong family team unless, of course, we use our in-laws to fill the gap.

For most of us, our own parents supply the most consistent and powerful grandparent resource. When this holds true for both members of a couple, the child can have four wonderful grandparents (and "bonus" great-grandparents as well). The value that we place on our relationship with our parents, and our desire to keep it healthy, increase our ability to enjoy one another and cope with problems.

For example, Sue, forty-three, is someone who values her parents and her in-laws. "I have wonderful parents, and they are wonderful grandparents. My husband agrees too. When problems come up, we have a sit-down, discuss them without emotional flare-ups, and resolve them. If my parents can't do it, my husband's can."

When parents don't value their own parents, it hinders their ability to call on them when needed. When I first met Santiago, thirty-three, he avoided his father and wanted to block him from his children. Santiago had a lot of resentment to overcome before he was able to get past his negative feelings and include his own father as a member of his family team. Initially, he wanted to be as far away from his father as possible. In his view, he had good reasons for feeling this way.

"All he did when I was young was to push me in school and cramp my social life. I had no childhood. My father was very critical.

I could never please him. I had to work seven days a week, five in school, then out in the fields afternoons and weekends. We never had any fun, everything was work. That's why I don't want to expose my kids to him. Of course, he has mellowed in his old age and wonders why I avoid him. I know he loves my kids too. I don't want him doing the same things to my kids, teaching them that life is a downer. So I don't get too close. My wife tells me to try, but I just can't forgive him. Everyone in my family is on my case about this."

As Santiago said, damage from the past is not easy to surmount. From the family team perspective, however, it is worth his effort to try to salvage whatever good he can from the negative experience and *make sure* that he does not repeat the same mistakes in future generations. With some help, Santiago eventually allowed his father more time with the children. He expressed amazement at how different his father was with the children.

"He is not the same person," Santiago said. "He is much nicer to my kids than he was to me. I guess I'll try to have a more positive attitude toward him. I think he knows the score and is reaching out to me a little more now that I've relented. But it ain't easy. Let me tell you."

Forgiving Past Mistakes

It's important for the success of our new family team and the well-being of our children that we try to heal any old wounds and give our parents an opportunity to make amends. Now that they are older and wiser, I am sure that given the opportunity, those who are able to do so will make the effort.

Phil, a seventy-six-year-old father of six, expresses what many grandparents feel: "I wish I was a father to young kids today. I made so many mistakes when I was a young father myself, errors I would never have committed if I had it to do over again. I feel so sad about all the good things I could have done for my kids. Less criticism. A kind word here, a hug. Now I know what these gestures mean. I didn't then. I am trying to make up for it now that they are older."

Consider how many of your unhappy experiences with your parents are still with you. How much do they affect your current attitudes and behaviors toward your parents? How do they affect your motivation to include them in your family team? What do your parents feel? Has anything changed over the years? Whatever your family history, consider getting together with your parents to review the past and address old issues with an eye toward healing.

Some have found it helpful to meet with their parents in a neutral setting (a walk in the park, a restaurant) and discuss their feelings and attitudes in an objective way. Resolving issues from the past can't happen when criticism, anger, and blame are wildly cast. Expressing hurt always gets a person's attention and elicits compassion. Understanding, reason, and tolerance are the watchwords. Overcoming any pain from the past is important when it comes to dealing with present and future conflicts and not entangling them in unresolved past issues.

Take a moment to consider the current state of your relationship with your own parents and in-laws. Identify any problem areas. These are issues that you might want to address with your own parents in the future as you proceed to right any wrongs of the past.

Guidelines for Moving Onward and Upward

Now we'll turn back to the present and the future. Here are some guidelines for you to use to help overcome any negative legacy from the past and to start anew to create and maintain your family team. These guidelines can be applied as both useful principles and flexible tools for prevention and conflict resolution.

1. *Start at the beginning: before you get married and before your child is born.* Begin at the beginning. Think "family team" with your own parents. Let your parents know that you and your partner want to get along as well as possible with them. Then make the effort to cultivate a good relationship with them and include them in your life. Let grandparents in on your decisions. Ask

for advice and counsel when appropriate. Make grandparents part of your life.

2. *Work hard at creating a healthy in-law relationship.* You can avoid many potential difficulties by developing a one-to-one *direct* relationship with each of your partner's parents, who are also your child's potential grandparents. Your efforts not only will make your partner happy but also will increase your partner's respect for you. As we've discussed earlier, no one wants to be caught between a partner and a parent. Your proactive efforts will be appreciated, and you will be rewarded by gaining status and respect in your in-laws' eyes. This is especially important if marital conflicts arise. Experience has shown that when a good parent-in-law relationship exists, it can continue even after a divorce. This is very beneficial to children, who feel that they do not have to choose between family members. When this happens, it also limits disputes and maintains generational continuity between a custodial parent and an in-law grandparent.

3. *Involve grandparents when the baby is on the way.* Having a baby is a family affair. A parent is supported when everyone on the family team is involved in the planning, even children. When you include the future grandparents in the process, you are paving the way for their relationship with your child (and you may more easily get any financial assistance you need—such as a new crib or stroller).

   I also recommend that you start a *family conference* tradition between you and all the future grandparents to coalesce the family ego and discuss the family hopes and dreams. Make clear what you need from them, and discuss your mutual ideas about how you would like your child to be raised. Setting the precedent for the family conference at this happy and exciting time is especially important. In the future, the family conference can serve as a forum in which to deal with conflicts as well.

4. *Continually monitor the health of your three-dimensional relationship.* Keep your finger on the pulse of your family—especially

between you and your parents and you and your in-laws. Also keep an eye on how the grandparents get along with one another. Talk with them about how things are going, identify any issues, and address them. Be sure to choose the right forum for discussion. Lunch is great! Don't be shy about mediating any issues between your child and grandparents too.

5. *Strive for good open, honest, and direct communication.* I cannot emphasize how important it is for you to be open and direct with each family member about your feelings. When you identify a need or an issue, call a get-together with the person involved. Once together (again choose the time and place well), openly, and respectfully, express your feelings, listen attentively to the other party's views, and express your desire to work toward a satisfactory resolution of the issue.

Never *triangulate*. (This means telling someone else your feelings before dealing directly with the person involved.) Be direct. If you have to vent, do so with a trusted person, one who is capable of maintaining strict confidence. Be warned, however, that for most human beings this is extremely difficult. Triangulation is one of the worst ways of dealing with conflict because it inevitably fans the flames of any family fire and spreads the danger to others.

6. *Be vigilant of your partner's relationship with your parents and children.* Never, never get caught in the middle of a fracas between your partner and your parents, or vice versa. That is why it is so important to discuss your family relations on a regular basis with your partner. When dealing with third parties, you want to be on the same side with your partner as often as possible. Then when conflicts arise, you will be able to deal with them together, as a family unit, rather than in a divided way.

Partner disagreement happens frequently with in-law problems. In this situation, it is imperative that both parents have thought through the issue and agree to a reasonable strategy for addressing and attempting to resolve any conflict. As mentioned earlier, it is especially important for your children to see you and your partner operate in such a considered, nonreactive manner.

7. *Know thyself: separate your own issues from your parents and children*. Be aware of the subjectivity of human experience. All this means is that others may not share your view of a specific issue or conflict. That is why it is important to objectify (as best you can) your thoughts and feelings before acting. So listen, listen, listen to others. It's helpful to ask others for feedback about a situation that you may not be sure about. Respect the fact that others may neither agree with you nor see things as you do. For example, if you are having a problem with grandparents, especially your own parents, your children may say that they agree with you, just to make you happy. Children caught in the middle of a parent-grandparent conflict tell both parties whatever they want to hear about who is right and who is wrong. Self-preservation is the name of their game. The same consideration extends to your partner, who may be having a conflict with your parents that you may want to ignore or minimize. Listen carefully to what your partner says, no matter how uncomfortable it makes you feel. Your partner may be right!

8. *Prepare the next generation: model mutual respect for your children*. Recognize and respect that you are preparing your child for a family future. The way you act toward your partner, parents, and in-laws will be copied by your child.

Justin, twelve years old, explains this well: "I like it when my parents and grandparents are nice to each other. When my mom is mad at my grandmother, I do not want to hear about it, because I am not mad at my grandmother. Actually, it makes me feel terrible. Mom should keep the grown-up stuff between the adults and not get us kids involved. When they do nice things for each other, it makes me feel warm and happy inside."

So keep the adult stuff between adults. Maintain mutual respect even in tough times, and your children will do the same. It's also rewarding to talk to your child about the idea of the family team and to show how to make it work. Felice, sixteen, said, "My dad is always talking with me about how important family is. He is so nice and respectful with my grandparents that it is a good example for me how to treat him when he gets old. I hope I can be as good a daughter as he is a son."

9. *Think grandparent! Bring grandparents into your everyday life.* Part of your job is to keep grandparents up-to-date on what it is like to run a family nowadays. So take them along to your place of work and your child's doctor visits. Invite them to your child's class, so they can get acquainted with modern methods of education. Discuss current events. Pass them articles relating to new and modern ways of child rearing. When you make them part of your daily life, you will have a greater knowledge and understanding of what their world is like too. As a bonus, you might bootleg a little one-to-one private attention for yourself as well.

10. *Call a time-out when conflicts occur.* It is important to contain the flames of conflict. When things get too hot, call a time-out, and suggest the same to everyone else involved. This is especially important to do where in-laws are concerned or other third parties are involved.

Azza, thirty-nine, got into an argument with her mother-in-law, who was baby-sitting her child. Her mother-in-law (without Azza's permission) had rearranged Azza's furniture when Azza was off to work. In Azza's culture, the mother-in-law is a powerful figure. Since Azza came over to the United States six years ago (in an arranged marriage), she noticed that her mother-in-law (who lived with them) was becoming increasingly controlling and "downright bossy." For Azza, however, changing around her furniture was "the last straw." "Sure she watches my child but what price do I have to pay? I have no privacy," she said.

When her husband, Khalil, came home that night, he got angry with both Azza and his mother. "What can I do?" he cried. "One of them has to go." So in the heat of battle, his mother left to go live with her sister.

"Good," said Azza, "but now I feel guilty. Khalil didn't take my side, so I want to leave too but I have no place to go."

Meanwhile Khalil was "fed up with these people. Why can't they get along? They all act like children, and I've got a business to run."

All this while, their child cried for hours. Azza might have avoided the spread of misery if she had taken a brief walk and sorted out her feelings after she saw her house "redecorated." Experience shows that awful things can be said in the heat of conflict, things that people don't really mean. Time-outs and cooldowns do work. They work with children too.

11. *Be cool; don't be reactive: think through your feelings, attitudes, views, and opinions before you intervene or state your position.* Time-outs act by curbing reactivity. This is not easy, to be sure, especially for those of us with emotional temperaments. Nevertheless always take time to reflect and examine all sides of a situation before responding or intervening. It's wonderful for your child to see you as patient and controlled. As Azza learned, reactivity—loss of cool—can convert temporary conflicts into long-term problems. Conflicts are more readily worked out when reason, not reactivity, prevails.

12. *Change places: put yourself in the other person's shoes.* When controversy arises, and you have successfully recognized and dealt with your emotions, then switch roles and put yourself in the other person's shoes. This is something that Azza failed to do. Try as best you can to view any conflict from the other person's perch. By so doing, you will be able to avoid a great deal of controversy and aggravation and at the same time offer a great example. This ability will not go unrecognized by your children.

13. *Be a peacemaker.* Although you don't want to let hot conflicts get out of control, you must let emotions be expressed. After a time-out, give people permission to express their feelings. When they do, listen in peace, don't react, and allow them to

vent everything until they are "empty." Although we shouldn't place much credence on what is said in the heat of emotions, we must consider carefully what is expressed with reason. Forgiveness is important too. It's always nice to ask an individual who blows off a lot of steam in the heat of the fray if he really meant what he said at the time. Give him a chance for an out and to edit his remarks. When a person is upset, the last thing we want to do is to retaliate or "cork" his feelings. "Listen and learn" is the best motto. Maybe he is right.

14. *Be aware that you are teaching your child by example, and keep the child out of the conflict.* Your child is watching everything you do—positive and negative. He will treat you in exactly the same way that he feels you are treating him. A positive model is permanent and worth the effort. You want your child to see you as a peacemaker and a healer. Do not neglect, however, to ask about your child's feelings regarding conflicts and issues that he experiences. Validating a child's feelings builds character and self-worth.

15. *Be aware of your future grandparenthood.* Here is the bottom line: At this very moment, you are setting the example for your child's future parenthood, and grandparenthood. You can begin to undo any damage of the past and start to teach your child what three-dimensional parent consciousness is all about—right now, today, and every day.

Part of the greatest legacy we can pass on to our child is to model our success in identifying, addressing, and resolving conflicts and problems. Learning to address and deal with conflict is the most important skill that we possess as a three-dimensional parent. In the following chapters, we'll see how conflicts occur and evolve and discuss the most frequent reasons and circumstances that cause conflicts between parents and grandparents.

5

Managing Family Conflicts

If parents want to manage a family team successfully, they must assume leadership of the group. Furthermore they must apply their leadership and act as a proactive, positive force for joy, meaning, and inspiration to family members. We must also be willing to grow and learn—to acquire the education and skills to be able to enhance family life as well as identify, address, and resolve conflicts. Success in the latter endeavor requires knowledge about the genesis and evolution of conflict and how it affects different situations and circumstances. With this information, we can manage conflicts with a clinical eye, augment our objectivity, and increase our chances of achieving success. Here is what you need to know.

The Origins of Family Conflict

A conflict is a disagreement between two or more people. Time has taught me that whether or not it is temporary or long-standing, every conflict passes through a sequence of stages as it runs its course.

A conflict often starts with a *trigger event*, which initiates the conflict: someone says or does something that offends another person. In response, the recipient of the real, or even perceived (in the cases of very sensitive people or misunderstandings), affront then reacts. Emotions are generated. If the will is there, a period of direct confrontation takes place, communication is achieved, and ideally a successful resolution follows. When people ignore the conflict and walk away from dealing with it directly, it becomes unresolved—that is, chronic. Unexpressed feelings simmer and turn to hurt and anger. Without confrontation and resolution, the parties have no recourse but to "shun" or avoid one another. Most often, other family members become involved and often become uncomfortable. When people line up against one another on different sides of the issue, a permanent breach may develop. In extreme cases, the family can come apart at the seams. Sadly, I have seen this happen.

The different conflicts that occur between parents and grandparents have many sources. They can arise from simple disagreements or misunderstandings concerning child-rearing ideas or religious differences—a clash of attitudes and viewpoints. More seriously, they may happen because of bad personal chemistry between people—that is, personalities that rub one another the wrong way.

For example, Mike, thirty-two, is a self-described "messy" person, who says he "can't stand my wife's mother because she is a compulsive neatnik." So Mike avoids her. Often the problems between parent and child (as parent and grandparent) are due to old resentments and unresolved parent-child issues, which I discussed in the preceding chapter.

For the most part, conflicts fall into two distinct categories: someone is doing something hurtful, or someone is not doing something helpful. Conflicts may occur through no one's fault, or they may be generated on purpose by someone's wanting to cause trouble. Irritating habits, as Mike describes, can cause conflicts through no one's fault. It is not his mother-in-law's fault that she is a neatnik. It's Mike's objections to her habits that cause the conflict. If he were able to live and let live, there would not be a problem unless his mother-in-law criticized him. In contrast, conflicts can be caused willingly—for example, when an injurious behavior is identified, and the offender does not want to change the behavior.

Rouella is a thirty-four-year-old mother who does not want her children to visit her own mother's house because grandma smokes cigarettes. In this instance, the grandmother is doing something that Rouella finds dangerous for her children. Rouella is justified in being concerned about her children's health. It is therefore appropriate to expect grandma to alter her behavior if she wants her grandchildren to visit. The conflict therefore is *grandma's fault*.

Communication or the lack thereof is an important factor in generating conflicts. Conflicts frequently occur when people are not open, direct, and clear with one another about their feelings and do not make the effort to communicate directly. This cannot be attributed to anyone's *fault*, but rather to an attitudinal, personality, situational, or lifestyle reason.

Alice, a sixty-four-year-old grandmother, did not want to get involved in her daughter's life, because she did not want, in her words, "to put my nose in their business. My mother put her nose in my business all of the time, and I do not want to do the same to my daughter." The mistake is that Alice *never asked* her daughter if she thought Alice was meddling. Alice just thought she was being sensitive. Eventually, after a family argument, Alice learned, to her bewilderment, that her daughter was actually sad and angry and felt abandoned by Alice and that the notion that Alice was meddling had never entered her mind.

The Danger of Communication Breakdown

Every conflict worsens when people can't communicate openly and directly with one another about the issue. Obviously, people cannot change their behaviors when they have no clue that what they are doing is hurtful to others.

Celia, twenty-eight, was upset because her mother had criticized her cooking in front of the family. In fact, the quality of Celia's cooking (lightheartedly acknowledged as bad) was a family joke. This made it worse for Celia, whose mother was an excellent cook. Celia went along with being lovingly ridiculed until one Sunday morning when she prepared lunch for her family and her parents after church. After her husband made a snide remark about the "rubberlike" consistency of her omelette, extracting chuckles from the other guests, Celia hurled the frying pan, containing a very large omelette, across the room and through the kitchen window.

Her husband and mother were stunned. Celia, openmouthed, was stunned as well! "My God, I never knew that her feelings were hurt," her husband said.

"I'll teach her better," Celia's mother said.

Celia said, "Now they know."

Differences in Attitude and Priorities

Personal differences in attitudes and values cause many conflicts between people who are competitive and cannot live and let live. A Republican parent with a Democratic in-law is an accident waiting to happen. Attitudinal differences that can place parents and grandparents on opposite sides of the fence of opinion are infinite. Here are some examples of touchy issues between parents and grandparents that I have come across:

Should a mother with a young child work?

Is co-sleeping appropriate?

Should dad be the primary caretaker?

How much time should a grandparent spend baby-sitting?

How much is a grandparent willing to help parents financially without resenting it?

The circumstances are endless because generations are raised in different times and different realities. When people can see no further than the borders of their experience and are unwilling—or unable—to consider another's point of view, the fur can fly.

Most parent-grandparent conflicts are temporary clashes arising from intergenerational differences in the way things should be done. Take co-sleeping, as I just mentioned, as an example of a common source of parent-grandparent disagreement today. Few of today's grandparents slept with their children. If they did, it was probably because they could not afford to do otherwise. When Consuelo, twenty-eight, gave birth to Juan and slept with him, her affluent parents argued endlessly with her.

"You might roll over on him in the middle of the night. How can you have a romantic life? You might squash the baby," her father said. "I can't sleep at night for worrying." Consuelo's mother, Bebe, fifty-four, could not understand why her daughter tolerated Juan crawling all over her at night and then complaining the next morning that she was exhausted and had to find time to nap during the day. In response, Consuelo said that all of her friends with children were co-sleeping as well. With time, this conflict too shall pass.

Extreme Conflict

In contrast, more serious conflicts that arise from lack of trust or respect, personal differences in values, objectionable behavior or even pathology, can crack the three-dimensional system apart by removing grandparents from the system. In recent years, extreme conflicts have led many parents to cut off grandparents from their families. In fact, many parents, because they are so angry about grandparents' behavior, have virtually legislated grandparents out of existence. Instead of getting rid of the problems with relatives, many get rid of the relatives.

Sometimes this is understandable, sometimes not. Getting rid of grandparents was easy before the 1970s because grandparents had no legal rights. Since then, *grandparent visitation laws* have been put in place to support grandparents' ability to petition for visitation with a grandchild in the case of parental death or divorce. Recently, some states have repealed these laws, citing parents' constitutional right to raise their child as they see fit—with or without grandparents.

Parents will always protect their children from pathological or destructive behavior, whoever is the culprit—even grandparents. Fortunately, however, most family conflicts inhabit a gray area of differences in attitudes, habits, and perceptions. Such issues can be readily repaired with understanding, tolerance, and good communication:

especially when parents learn and apply some of the skills and tools for dealing with conflicts that I describe in the following discussion.

The Dynamics of Conflicts

Conflicts are normal and expected. It is how we deal with them that determines their positive or negative outcome. First, here's a brief rundown of how conflicts unfold:

- *Trigger.* An event precipitates the conflict.
- *Reaction.* The parties react to the problem. They become defensive.
- *Judgment and faultfinding.* Blame is spread around. It is usually the other person's fault.
- *Choosing sides.* The parties seek validation and allies.
- *Open warfare.* Emotions are expressed; the fur flies.
- *Successful outcome: confrontation.* The problem is addressed and resolved.
- *Unsuccessful outcome: estrangement.* The parties do not openly identify the issue and deal with it. The issue is sidestepped. Shunning or avoidance occurs and feelings fester.

To avoid an unsuccessful outcome, remember that if the issue is never addressed, people become estranged from one another. We all know of people who hold grudges and who have not spoken to the other for decades over an incident long past. In many cultures, these unresolved problems are at the root of family feuds, some that persist through many generations.

Managing Conflicts

You can both prevent and repair conflicts. Here are some systematic guidelines for how to proceed. You can apply this procedure to any of the variety of conflicts that you encounter, whether you are directly involved or the conflict is between other members of your family team. In the next chapters, I will enumerate a number of common conflicts that parents encounter with grandparents and show how these guidelines can be successfully applied to help.

- *Assess the situation.* When the conflict occurs, think before reacting. What is happening and who is involved? What is the trigger event? Is someone obviously at fault?

- *Determine how "hot" the conflict is.* Is open warfare occurring? Are feelings not being expressed or addressed and lie simmering below the surface? Are the parties triangulating—complaining to others rather than to one another? Are family members choosing up sides?

- *Evaluate the status.* What is the conflict about? Is it a temporary disagreement that will soon blow over of its own accord? Is it part of a more severe, chronic, and deep-seated conflict? (Are the parties shunning one another, or are they estranged?)

- *Identify the people and positions.* What are the stories and attitudes of the people involved in the conflict? Are they flexible or intractable? Can they put themselves in one another's shoes?

- *Engage in self-examination.* What are your own thoughts, feelings, and behavior about the conflict and the people involved? Are you helping or hurting the situation? If you are not directly involved (for example, if the conflict is between your partner and your parent, or your child and a grandparent), are you being neutral?

- *Begin communication.* Open the channels of communication. Talk to the parties involved and listen to their views. When people cannot talk to one another, appoint a family peacemaker.

- *Analyze.* Analyze the problem with the involved parties. Avoid prejudgment. Are different lifestyles, personalities, or attitudes the root of the problem? Is there a clear "guilty" party?

- *Establish common ground.* Define the common interests of the parties involved.

- *Agree on a plan of action.* Based on your common interests, discuss the best available options to resolve the problem. Then formulate a plan that everyone can agree to.

- *Implement the plan.* Do what is necessary to bring the parties together and make a commitment for healing.

- *Do a follow-up.* If necessary, have periodic meetings with the involved parties to monitor, discuss, and improve the plan.

- *Forgive, forget, and make up.* This is the essential ingredient, heralding the demise of the conflict.

- *Remember prevention.* Identify and address conflicts before they grow out of control. This is the most effective way of maintaining family harmony. Keep in mind that even the stickiest problems can usually be resolved by means of early identification, direct communication, open discussion, and continual monitoring.

- *Get outside help.* If you can't do it alone, steer the parties to outside professional help.

- *Document the outcome in memory.* You might want to tell your grandchildren how you worked out the problem.

Although some degree of conflict with grandparents is inevitable, most conflicts can be successfully resolved. When this happens, everyone changes for the better, and relationships achieve a higher plane of love and understanding and tolerance.

Forgiveness is not just an important personal quality. It is also an important ingredient in the mortar that binds the family team together. Parents and grandparents owe it to their children to do whatever it takes to reconcile their differences. In the next chapter, I will show you how these guidelines can be applied to a broad variety of family situations, some of which you may have already encountered.

6

Personal Conflicts

Conflict, in one form or another, contains the seeds of growth. Family conflicts, therefore, although they may be emotionally unpleasant, can offer us an opportunity to stretch our tolerance, understanding, and capacity to forgive and forget—and grow personally as a result. Indeed when disagreements are addressed and resolved, the mutual respect and understanding that results brings the parties closer. It is therefore worth our effort to look at any conflict that we encounter as a source of learning and positive change. It further behooves us to take the time to become skilled at identifying, preventing, and dealing with the different types of conflicts that we will inevitably encounter during our lifetime.

The types of conflict that I have personally and professionally observed between parents and grandparents may be classified into two groups. The first group contains differences in personality and temperament. The types of conflict in the second group are generated by situations and circumstances that stress relationships. In the next two chapters, I will highlight some of the most common subjects of conflict that we are all likely to encounter in both groups. Some will be relevant to you personally, because no one is spared. Here's a brief preview:

- Personal grandparent issues leading to conflicts
    Temperament and personality

Poor boundaries

Self-centeredness (narcissism)

- Situational and circumstantial grandparent issues leading to conflicts

Lifestyle and attitude conflicts—spoiling, favoritism, discipline, competing grandparents, too much grandparenting, too little grandparenting (grandparent deprivation)

Family rearrangements—divorce, remarriage, stepparenting and stepgrandparenting, grandparent divorce

Family diversity—race, religion, gay and lesbian issues (gay and lesbian parents or gay and lesbian grandparents)

Here's a brief caution before we proceed: I have categorized the topics of conflict for the purpose of easier understanding. Because it is so easy for some to attach labels to people, I would not want these categories to be used in a pejorative way. For example, calling a grandparent a "narcissistic grandparent" (thereby using the category as a pejorative label)—true as it may be for purposes of understanding—won't help the grandparent stop the behavior. Indeed it may hurt feelings to a point where the person feels so insulted and alienated that he or she no longer wants to be involved in a healing process.

Although each category that I discuss stands alone as a unique type of behavior, it often coexists with another type of behavior. For example, a grandparent who does "too much" may also be insensitive to the parent's needs, ignore family boundaries, and have a narcissistic (self-centered) personality. When a situational conflict occurs (such as divorce or remarriage), such a grandparent might be useless to help, likely being more concerned about his or her own feelings than that of family members going through the divorce.

Grandparent Personality Issues

Any conflict that we encounter will be affected by the basic nature—personality—of the people involved. In its turn, the personality of an individual depends greatly on that person's temperament. Every grandparent that we deal with—our parents and our in-laws—just like everyone else, comes packaged with a "temperament" as standard equipment, and attention must be paid to it. In order to keep our family team hale and hearty, we have to learn how to deal with different temperamental types. Here are some of the most important points about temperament that everyone needs to know.

Technically speaking, temperament is an aspect of individual personality that affects our emotional and psychological makeup. Our temperament determines, for the most part, our reflexive patterns of thinking, behaving, and reacting. There are many varieties of temperament. For example, take a moment to study the temperamental types of your family and friends. Notice how some seem full of life and enthusiasm, whereas others are more laid-back or even lethargic. Some talk incessantly, and others rarely speak unless spoken to. You may have one relative who is a reserved intellectual and another who is constantly in motion and hates to read. Someone in your family may be a "party person" that keeps your family laughing, whereas another one is a confirmed grouch.

Temperament constitutes an important part of what we describe as our personality. Simply put, we describe people with an outgoing personality as *extroverts*. Such folks are usually articulate, enjoy socializing, and have a good sense of humor. Those with an inward personality we call *introverts*, and they prefer solitude and limited social activity. All of us possess a unique mixture of diverse temperamental traits that influence us in a variety of ways. Moreover temperament style can be an asset or a liability, depending on the circumstances. It all depends on central casting.

For example, a passive, intellectual type would do better in a university than working at a building site. For a physical, outgoing, and hearty person, working as a building contractor might be a great job. People who share similar temperaments attract one another and tend to get along well. The opposite is also true: people with dissimilar temperaments may rub one another the wrong way or even antagonize one another. The old adage that "opposites attract" may be true in love, but the converse, "opposites repel," is true as well and may also be aptly applied to those looking for a good brawl.

Psychiatrists Alexander Thomas and Stella Chess are pioneers in the field of temperament.[1] They categorized nine different types of temperament that can be useful for you to know as you deal with grandparents and others. In listing these types, I have included some questions. Your answers will give you a hint about your own type of temperament.

- *Activity level.* How active or passive are you? Are you a morning person or a night person? Are you full of pep or lackadaisical?

- *Regularity of patterns.* Are your work, eating, sleeping, and other habits orderly or chaotic? Are regularity and consistency important to you?

- *Approach or withdrawal.* Do you respond to new situations with hesitancy and reluctance or with enthusiasm?

- *Adaptability.* Are you resistant to change or easily adaptable to new situations?

- *Threshold of responsiveness.* Do you react quickly to new situations, or does it take awhile for you to respond? Do you hide your feelings?

- *Intensity of reaction.* Are you emotional, responding with much feeling, or are you unresponsive?

- *Quality of mood.* Are you an up person—optimistic and cheerful—or are you pessimistic and slow to warm up to people?

- *Distractibility.* Does your mind bounce from subject to subject, or can you stay focused for a long period? Are you highly organized or laissez-faire?

- *Attention span and persistence.* Do you have difficulty listening to others without losing attention? Do you have trouble sticking to a task until completion?

From this constellation of traits, three temperamental *clusters* have been identified, which may be used to categorize individuals as *easygoing, hard to get along with,* or *takes a long time to get to know.* For example, people who are approachable, relate easily, and are energetic and optimistic are *easy.* Others who are shy, pessimistic, agitated, or always moving or talking may be more *difficult* to relate to. Those who are slow to adapt to new situations, do not like change, and have a low level of responsiveness are *slow to warm up.* Of course, this has nothing to do with being a good, kind, and loving person.

We can use these categories as a useful tool to help us understand any temperamental difference we may have with a grandparent. After reading the preceding discussion, how would you categorize your temperament? How would you describe the temperaments of the grandparents you deal with? Are they similar or different from yours? Are you easy with one another, or do you tend toward rubbing one another the wrong way from time to time? Most important, do your temperaments "fit" with one another or not? If they do not, care is needed.

Dealing with Differences in Temperament

I cannot overemphasize the importance of the *fit factor.* If your type of temperament fits with grandparents, chances are, you will get along smoothly (as long as there are no external circumstances that divide you). This holds true whether you are a biological parent, an adoptive parent, or a stepparent.

As Phyllis, thirty-three, said, "My mother-in-law and I are like peas in a pod—quiet and shy. My husband said that's why he married me. She likes to quilt. So do I. And my oldest daughter, Sarah, nine, is just like us. So we have a great time quilting together."

The converse is true too. An exaggerated dose of a particular personality characteristic or a polar opposite (shy versus outgoing, noisy versus retiring) can lead to trouble. An overemotional grandparent (tending toward the *hysterical*, in psychological terms) may tend to overreact or worry too much in the eyes of an even-tempered parent. A slightly paranoid grandparent, expressing fear and caution too often, may frighten a child and irritate parents. A parent who is a laissez-faire housekeeper is heading for trouble with a compulsively neat mother-in-law, unless they can live and let live.

Take, for example, Lara, forty-five, and her mother, Vera, sixty-seven. "Oil and water, that's what we are," says Lara. "She likes bland food. I like spicy food. She likes classical music. I like jazz, and she hates jazz. She's a conservative; I am a libertarian. It never ends. Otherwise we get along."

Vera laughed, "If I didn't see Lara come out of me, I wouldn't believe she was my daughter. What a character. We argue all of the time, and I have to walk on eggs around her. Thank God we are *so* different, all we can do is laugh about it . . . at least some of the time."

Because temperamental differences can cause conflicts, it is important to pay attention to our fit with grandparents. When there is a personality, temperament, or personal-interest difference (like Lara and Vera), watch out for trouble. The best intervention is prevention. We need to identify potential areas of conflict quickly.

Take, for example, Irving, a thirty-five-year-old father of two and a stock market day trader. Irving prevented a possible conflict by making it clear to his retired, but active and athletic, father-in-law that Irving was a card-carrying "couch potato, computer nerd" and was not at all interested in playing active sports such as golf or tennis with him. When his father-in-law kept urging him to get involved in a sport, Irving told him, in a respectful and humorous way, "Hey, I'm a slug, but take my kids with you anytime, and play whatever you want." Irving's pronouncement made his children happy, his father-in-law very happy, and allowed Irving to go back to his computer "in peace." Here is Irving's formula for success:

- He acknowledged the temperamental and interest differences between his father-in-law and him in a warm and humorous way.

- He was neither critical nor defensive.

- He was respectful of their differences and gave them permission to be themselves.

- He respected their right to fulfill their own temperamental imperatives.

- He respected the grandparent-grandchild bond and allowed his children and his father-in-law to share their interests.

Live and Let Live

When we identify differences, we should not make the common mistake of judging or criticizing others for their temperament type. Temperament is destiny. There's nothing much we can do about it. Like Irving, we must respectfully accept people the way they are made and accept the differences with an open heart. Criticizing others will most often drive them away and set a bad example.

Joy, thirty-five, a rather flamboyant mother with a New Age taste, poked fun at her traditional mother-in-law, Paula, sixty-six (behind Paula's back). Paula liked to collect small glass table decorations and Hummel figures, which Joy thought were "old-fashioned and ugly." Ritchie, Joy's eight-year-old son, who loves Joy dearly, let the cat out of the bag and told grandma Paula that his mom thought she had "weird" taste. Hurt, and disappointed, Paula shunned Joy for many weeks. Joy, confused about Paula's aloofness, finally found out what had happened, after her husband asked Paula to explain her behavior. Joy went over to Paula and apologized for "shooting off my mouth." Joy's mistake was not allowing others to live and let live.

Here are some guidelines for dealing with conflicts that are rooted in temperamental differences:

- Know yourself first. Assess your own temperament in terms of its assets and liabilities. Where do you fit in the categories mentioned previously?

- Get an idea of each grandparent's temperament.

- Are you an easy fit? If not, where are the differences?

- Make the necessary adjustments in the light of this new awareness.

- If you find yourself getting tense around someone, take a time-out. Increase the distance between you and the other person for a while.

- Be aware of any temperamental changes with growth. Age and circumstance can affect temperament. Because people grow and change, often for the better, be alert to the fact that your fit might change too.

- Set a good example. Teach everyone in the family about temperament, announce your own temperamental liabilities, and let your family know how you manage its challenges. Use humor too. Being funny sets a great example!

Boundary Issues

Boundaries between generations delineate their different roles and responsibilities. When grandparents do not respect such boundaries and invade the regions of parental authority, responsibility, and control, conflict is inevitable. When the first child comes along, the former parent-child boundaries undergo a radical change. A new parent-grandparent component is added. New roles and identities are assumed. Adjustment to these new roles and responsibilities is often not easy, even for the most resilient among us.

First-time parents are especially and understandably insecure and defensive about their new responsibilities. The process of adjustment makes us vulnerable to conflicts because different people adjust to change at different speeds and can easily fall out-of-sync with one another. A new parent does not want to be treated as a child any longer. Often it takes time for a new grandparent to realize that and then act accordingly.

Fortunately, routine conflicts can be resolved with time, effort, maturity, and flexibility. When Kim, twenty-six, became a mother, her own mother, Margie, fifty-three, had no problem (in her words) "backing off and letting Kim take over. That's what my mother did for me. That's what I will do for Kim. She knows where I am if she needs me."

"That's right," said Kim. "I know where she is if I need her. She knows I have to make my own mistakes. She thinks I can do it all of the time. But she treats me like a child. She worries. I guess that's OK. At least she is trying." Kim is lucky to have a mother who respects her boundaries and her right to make her own mistakes as she tests out her newfound motherhood.

Margie says, "Seeing my baby as a mother is something else. It's hard to hold back."

In contrast, when grandparents do not respect generational boundaries, whether it is due to a lack of confidence in their child or to their own anxious personality (or other reasons), they can impair their child from becoming a responsible parent. This can be especially disastrous for a vulnerable or insecure parent, who needs support and praise to boost confidence.

For example, Lil, Pete, and their two youngsters used to live two floors below Pete's parents, Joan and Jim. Lil and Pete complained that the grandparents gave them no peace and acted as if they had no confidence in them as parents. "They rush down the two flights of stairs between our apartments at breakneck speed whenever they hear one of the kids cry. They constantly check up on us and pop in at all times of the day to play with the kids. They check what they eat and if they go to the bathroom every day."

Pete is especially perturbed that "my kids have more fun with my parents than with me. I never had that much fun with my parents. I have very mixed feelings about the whole thing. When I come home from work and my parents are around, the kids all but ignore me." Pete told his parents not to come on the weekends unless he asked them to because he wants time alone with his children. His parents were "deeply hurt" when he said this to them. Unfortunately, his parents couldn't listen, nor could they contain themselves from "barging in." As a result, he and his family moved a mile away to, in his words, "have some control over my parents' enthusiasm."

It is important to mention that some parents can equally overstep the grandparents' boundaries. Sometimes this is welcomed by grandparents, other times not. Pearl, twenty-five and a single mother, makes "constant demands" on her working mother, Sami, forty-nine and a registered nurse, to baby-sit her two young children on nights and weekends. They live together in a small house. Pearl, who was never married, works during the day and places her children in a day-care center. On nights and weekends, Pearl often stays out late, and on several occasions she stayed out all night (although she called Sami). In spite of Sami's pleading for Pearl to stay home more often and give Sami some free time, Pearl continued in her ways.

One day, Sami said, "I put my time in as a mother, and now I only want to be a grandmother, not the mother. You are the mother, Pearl, now act like one." Pearl, furious, responded that if Sami would not baby-sit, she would move out and that Sami couldn't see the grandchildren anymore. Much to the horror of Pearl's two sisters and brother, Pearl moved out to a boyfriend's house. Their standoff continued for three years, until Pearl remarried. Sadly, the separation caused the children to lose the close relationship they had with Sami.

In hindsight, Pearl realized that she had not assumed her parenting duties, had nudged Sami into the parenting role, and had acted essentially like an older sister to her children. Although sometimes this arrangement may be necessary, it works best when boundaries are maintained and the grandparent is clearly *supplementary* to whatever a parent can do at the time. As we will see in Chapter Eleven, this is the *family team method*, which works well if a parent is incapacitated and grandparents have to help.

Narcissism

Simply put, narcissism is self-centeredness coupled with immaturity. Narcissistic people see themselves as "the belly button of the universe" (as one young father described his own high-achieving father). Narcissistic people take most things personally. Narcissism is a normal condition in youngsters, who are naturally self-centered because they are actively building a self. As far as adults are concerned, we would hope that once they have matured, they can move on from being "selfish" to becoming "selfless"—and can put the needs of younger people before their own. But it doesn't always happen that way, and many adults of all ages remain to some degree immature and narcissistic.

Narcissism can be readily plotted on a continuum, ranging from zero narcissism (sainthood), to average self-interest (fighting your partner for the movie you want to see or battling for the TV remote control), to severe narcissism, which is total self-centeredness. Severe narcissism is a *personality disorder* that inhibits normal functioning and normal relationships. Its characteristic signs are self-importance, attention getting, insensitivity to others, a sense of entitlement, and a lack of empathy—in sum, self-centeredness. Severely narcissistic people can generate lots of conflict. Here is one extreme example of how a very narcissistic grandmother created havoc with two young parents.

Isabel, twenty-four, and Robert, twenty-seven, were overjoyed when their daughter, Catherine, was born. But whenever May, Robert's forty-nine-year-old mother, came over to see her granddaughter, she was taken aback that Catherine was often crying, not sleeping, and clinging to Isabel. The baby was colicky and having trouble nursing, so when May tried to hold Catherine, she began to cry. May, feeling rejected by the child, took this personally, saying that Catherine didn't like her. She began to criticize Isabel, who was already beside herself with worry, for Catherine's behavior.

Now most grandparents would have easily recognized and understood the baby's and the parent's confusion and suffering and would have offered to help. Not so with May. Being narcissistic, the frustration and disappointment that she felt about the child's inability to relate to her escalated into irritability. Unable to perceive how others feel, she became irritated with Isabel, holding her responsible for "having something wrong with your milk." This grandmother was more concerned about herself, and her frustration about not getting the love and adoration that she wanted from little Catherine, than she was about Catherine and Isabel going through a hard time. This is not very grandmotherly.

As a result, Isabel not only had Catherine's colic to deal with, but she also had, in her words, "another baby to deal with," with May. Fortunately, most of Robert's sisters and brothers (two of each) and his father were all well acquainted with May's antics. At Robert's request, they were able to support Isabel during Catherine's rough first year of life. Isabel's own mother was very helpful too.

As Catherine grew, she established a superficial relationship with May, who said (in private, to her credit), "I never took to Catherine."

Catherine began to feel that her grandmother didn't like her. When she talked to Isabel about her feelings, Isabel explained the situation in a kind way: "Well, dear, your grandmother loves you, but she just has a hard time showing it." Just imagine what Isabel would have gone through if she were a single parent and had only May to count on!

Even with family and partner support, dealing with a narcissistic grandparent is no cup of tea, especially if it is an in-law. What we never want to do is blame our partner for a parent's narcissism. Our partner needs support, having had plenty of personal misery dealing with such a parent, and already feels guilty about inflicting a narcissistic parent on us in the first place. Remember, we stay united with our partner at all costs. Narcissistic people like to divide and conquer.

Dealing with such conflicts tests the borders of our own tolerance, love, and understanding. Sometimes the best we can do is damage control: limiting contact with difficult grandparents or having contact with them under controlled circumstances. Getting together with them while other people are present is one good strategy. They can be with the grandchildren, and at the same time, we can relate to them in short bursts, consistent with our ability to tolerate them. In this way, we can allow our child to profit as much as possible under the circumstances.

Compromise, tolerance, and nonreactivity are the watchwords when dealing with a narcissistic grandparent. We need to use our ingenuity to extract any possible good from the relationship. We need to do our best to see to it that the grandchild-grandparent relationship continues as best as possible under the circumstances. We also have to keep in mind that our child might not be having the same difficulties with a narcissistic grandparent that we have.

One teenager, Kylane, fourteen, that I knew was well aware that her grandmother was narcissistic and tried to make the best of it. "She takes me to her country club and shows me off to her friends. Otherwise she doesn't pay much attention to me," she said. "I feel like I am only a charm on her bracelet. But she does buy me nice clothes, and I do get to go to the pool at the club and meet nice kids. So it's not that bad."

Since time began, parents and grandparents have lived in different times. Such differences in situations and circumstances can cause conflicts because of changing attitudes, lifestyles, and values. In the next chapter, I will explain some of these situations and circumstances and how they affect us, and I will discuss how to deal with the conflicts they cause.

7

Situational and Circumstantial Conflicts

How do we keep our family team together if we have to deal with personal and social situations and circumstances that cause conflicts in our relationships with grandparents? How do we live with and expose our children to grandparents who have personal habits, attitudes, and lifestyles that we may not agree with?

There are no easy answers to these questions. Each situation and circumstance has to be individually addressed. One thing we must do when we wrestle with such conflicts is to avoid throwing the baby out (in this case the grandparent) with the bathwater. But we also do not want to expose ourselves, nor do we want to expose our child, to excessive aggravation and even harm.

For example, Nicole, twenty-seven, calls herself a "New Ager." She is a massage therapist and fitness teacher, who is very upset with her mother's "bad" smoking habits. "My mother is a good person but smokes like a chimney. And every night, she and my dad drink a few too many beers. I tell them that their behavior worries me. But do they do anything about it? No!" Nicole continues, "They love my kids and want them to spend the night, but I can't allow my kids to get lung cancer, can I? My mother even lets the kids sip on a beer. She says a little beer is good for them and teaches the kids a good way to drink, with family. She says I am a fuddy-duddy and a health nut and that she is just having fun being a grandmother. She says her grandmother did the same with her. But that was before we knew about lung cancer. How can I leave my kids with them?"

Reaching the end of her rope, Nicole issued her parents an ultimatum: quit your smoking and giving the kids sips of beer, or no more visits. They could only see them at Nicole's house. Because Nicole was so determined and clear with her demands, the grandparents "cleaned up their act," as Nicole said.

Moreover grandma is now using a nicotine patch. "Maybe Nicole's right. I want to see my grandchildren," she said, "but it isn't easy. I'll try with the smoking but the beer stays."

Of course, when grandparents are involved in any reckless or life-threatening behavior or are undermining parents, it is right for parents to take a "time-out" and restrict their children's visits. It doesn't end there, however. Once a moratorium is declared, the issue should then be identified, discussed, and resolved. Most grandparents will come around to a parent's way of thinking and recognize a parent's deep concern when their relationship with a grandchild is at stake.

The following sections discuss some of the most common situations that cause parent-grandparent conflicts. They range from simple misunderstandings to complex differences. They concern spoiling, favoritism, attitudes and discipline styles, competing or feuding grandparents, differences in lifestyle or religious and ethnic values, too much grandparenting, and too little grandparenting— grandparent deprivation.

Understanding Grandparent Spoiling

As parents, we set the rules for raising our child. When grandparents go against our rules, "stretch" them a bit, or allow our child to diminish, even break, our rules and values, we get annoyed. How we see such infractions is relative (remember temperament?), so some of us may take such infractions more seriously than others of us do. Often what can be funny and frivolous for a grandparent and grandchild can be irritating to a concerned parent, who may view their antics as a threat to parental respect and authority.

"I don't want my daughter to see any PG movies yet, but my father takes her anyway. He spoils her rotten," complains Juliet, thirty-six. "He never treated me like he treats her. When it comes to my daughter, my father doesn't have the word no in his vocabulary."

Fortunately, most of us are understanding and are not bothered too much when our parents indulge our child. Many of us even enjoy it vicariously, especially if we had a great time with a grandparent of our own when we were young. Most of us respect the fact that a grandparent's natural instinct to spoil a grandchild is deep-rooted. Our role with our child is different. Although we love our child deeply, there is a burden and responsibility attached to this love. We are always teaching and training our child to survive and be competent in the world. Consequently, because our child wants to please us, he or she perceives that a portion of our parental love will be given or withdrawn according to our approval of the child's behavior.

Approval and rejection, praise and punishment, are built-in "conditions" for a child's relationship with its parents. As Selma, a six-year-old, said, "Mommy loves me when I am a good girl and gets mad when I do bad things." Grandparents get off easy because they don't have this responsibility with a grandchild, although they have it with us as our parents. Parenting and grandparenting are truly different.

That's why, however we feel, the best thing to do is to give our child and grandparents a long leash and try to enjoy their fun ourselves. But there is a tricky spin to all this as far as some parents are concerned. The fun can be so great for our child and our parents that—believe it or not—some parents can actually feel jealous.

Carolyn, thirty-four, expresses a bit of "grandparent envy." She wishes that her parents would treat her as well as they treat her child. "I'm envious of all the fun they have. My son gets whatever he wants, whenever he wants it. I know it sounds stupid to say it, and it is funny, but I wish they would treat me the same way. Let's face it. I am jealous. Although I don't like to feel this way, I actually resent them having such a good time."

Carolyn's dad explained that he is not the same person today as he was before. "I'm more laid-back in my old age, not as strict. My father was the same way. When he got to be a grandfather, he was a changed man. Runs in the family, I guess."

Fun is fun. However, some grandparents can abuse their license to indulge children. When a parent feels uncomfortable, it is time to intervene. Cara, twenty-eight, is angry with her in-laws because she feels that they are abusing their "spoiling rights."

"A little bit of spoiling is OK, but my mother-in-law oversteps her bounds. She gives my daughter, who has a weight problem, things I don't want her to have—like muffins, brownies, and pies. Would you believe it? She bakes her pies! My mother-in-law is a great baker but she overdoes it. She tells me that it makes her happy to bake goodies for my daughter. When I tell my daughter not to eat the fattening food at granny's house, she gets upset. Then I am the bad guy. My mother-in-law is heavy too. She feels that she is only doing what her grandmother did and what a grandmother is supposed to do—stuff my daughter's face. But I feel there is a limit and I've reached it."

Fortunately, Cara handled the conflict by getting a diet plan from their doctor and making a list of foods that her daughter was allowed to eat. Because there was medical authority backing up Cara's list, grandma followed the rules—well, most of the time.

When parents and grandparents don't get along well, spoiling can be a flash point for conflict. This happens when parents who have issues with their own parents view them behaving in a more generous and kindly way with their children. This can easily rekindle old resentments. If this is something you are experiencing, try to cut grandparents some slack, if only for the child's sake. There is a good reason for this. Being indulgent with our child gives our parents an opportunity to make up for what they think they did wrong with us.

It is all about restitution. As grandparents age, they come to realize the mistakes they made as parents. Some are eager to make up for their mistakes and do better for their family. Grandchildren are the natural beneficiaries of this benevolence. For some of us, it is like having different parents. Indeed this change in attitude and behavior can be bewildering and even hurtful if grandparents were formerly strict or not much fun. This change in demeanor is especially hard to bear for parents who felt deprived as children and harbor resentment. Understandably, it can make such a parent feel envious and hurt, especially if the grandparent seems exclusively focused on enjoying the grandchild and does not seem interested in spreading the joy to the parent.

Abusing Spoiling Privileges

On the other extreme, grandparents abuse their spoiling privilege when they break parental rules. Sometimes this behavior represents the tip of the iceberg of a deeper conflict. Tessie, a sixty-seven-year-old grandmother, feels that she is being punished, because her son has threatened to stop her granddaughter, Roselle, just turned twelve, from visiting her overnight.

"So I let Roselle stay up until midnight with me, and her parents want her in bed by ten. We had to finish our monopoly game. She loves it. True, when she went home the next morning, she was tired, but we had a great time. She can make up her sleep. Now my son won't let her stay overnight anymore."

Her son, Bryan, forty-three, said that spoiling his daughter was only the tip of the iceberg: the iceberg being that his mother never listens to him. "I told my mother to stick to my daughter's bedtime because she needs her sleep, and if she doesn't get her ten hours, she is knocked out for days. But does my mother listen? No way. And it's not only bedtime that is involved. It's food, and it's letting Roselle do whatever she wants."

I suggested to Bryan that what Tessie was doing didn't seem that bad. Especially if Roselle was having fun. "No," he said, "give her an inch and she'll take a mile. If my mother listened in other ways, it would be easier, but she is the most stubborn person I ever met. The only control I have is not to let Roselle stay overnight."

Indeed Bryan did stop Roselle's weekend visits with Tessie for three weeks. Then he relinquished. A chastened Tessie said, "He got me. I'll behave."

Because children have so much fun being spoiled, and because time, attention, and fun may be hard to come by in these purposeful times, a little spoiling won't hurt. We need to set the boundaries and then turn the other cheek when they are stretched—within reason, of course. There is a fine line between cute and serious. Naturally, if there is danger involved, or if grandparents go too far over the line, intervention is necessary.

Spoiling may also be manifested by an overwhelming urge by grandparents to lavish gifts on a grandchild. When this urge is not coordinated with parents' discretion and channeled in the right direction, it can cause problems. I will explain what can happen in detail in Chapter Ten when I discuss the financial aspects of the parent-grandparent relationship and explain what I have learned about the grandparent "buying bug."

Favoritism

Every grandchild should be a favorite, but that is not often the case. In fact, one of the most annoying things that parents can experience is when a grandparent favors one child over another. The favored child may be a sibling or may be a grandchild from the parent's sibling's family. Whatever the case, it's no fun for anyone except the anointed child. Generally, people who tend to favor one grandchild over another are responding to something in the "chosen one" that they have in common. Genes may be one thing. Grandchildren carry one-quarter of their grandparent's genes. A genetic resemblance may be expressed in similar physical or temperamental traits or may endow both with similar tastes, attitudes, or talents. As one grandfather put it, "Let's face it, don't we all like some people better than others? It's going to be the same with grandchildren, isn't it?"

A grandparent may also favor a certain grandchild because they share a common quality—for example, being the same gender; being the youngest or oldest child; having similar personality traits, physical characteristics, or talents. It can be intelligence, musicality, or athletic ability—whenever a grandchild is a chip off the grandparent's block. The grandparents that I know who single out a grandchild for extra attention say they "fit" well in some way or another with their grandchild (see the explanation of "fit" in Chapter Six).

Whether or not playing favorites ignites a conflict depends on the people and the circumstances. For example, the first grandchild is always everyone's favorite. There is no problem because there is no competition. When there are other grandchildren available, we need to make sure that all children are fairly treated. If you spot a grandparent playing favorites, intervene, even if it is happening to a sibling's child.

A favorite example of mine concerns Rebecca, thirty-five, who had to stop her own mother, Lottie, fifty-nine, from playing favorites. Lottie describes herself as being "crazy to a fault" about Evelyn, her four-year-old granddaughter. When the family is together, Lottie all but ignores Evelyn's older sister and brother. When Lottie arrives at Rebecca's house for a visit, she brings one present each for the other children and five for Evelyn, and she never misses bringing Evelyn her favorite chocolate éclair. "I can't help it," Lottie says, "I am nuts about Evelyn. I see myself in her. I try to help myself. The love just bursts out. Of course, I love the other children, but Evelyn will always be my number one grandchild."

Naturally, Rebecca feels protective of her other children. So she took action in a way that credits her three-dimensional outlook on her family: she wanted to get rid of the problem and not Lottie. So she invited Lottie out to lunch, where, in her words, she "read my mom the riot act, as sweetly as I could," Rebecca said. "I told her that her love affair with Evelyn was hurting the other children's feelings and that the children were starting to resent Evelyn. That got mom's attention. I almost made a mistake but I knew it and backed off. I almost started telling mom that she had also played favorites among *her* children. Fortunately, I was one of the chosen. However, I backed off because that would have been off the main subject."

Because of Rebecca's diplomatic and forthright effort, Lottie started treating all of the children "exactly" equal. "I still feel the same way," Lottie said, "but I don't show it. Evelyn is a bit disappointed being out of the spotlight. I don't like to be corrected, but

I didn't know how much my behavior was hurting Rebecca, and actually, I am proud of the way she told me off."

Although favoritism may seem a benign, or "cute," issue to grandparents, it is important for the "unfavored" child's sake to identify and correct the situation. It's important to nip favoritism in the bud because its negative effects can be exacerbated in situations such as adoption, divorce and remarriage, stepgrandparenting, or even when grandparents divorce or remarry.

Styles of Discipline

It is rare to find both parents and grandparents in total agreement over the way to raise a child. Most parents want to make sure not to repeat the errors of their own parents, as they raise their child. There is therefore a tendency for those of us who were raised strictly to be more permissive. If we were raised frugally, we may tend to have loose purse strings, and so on. Chances are, our children will repeat the cycle. This said, one of the most contentious areas of conflict between parents and grandparents is their different attitudes toward discipline and child-rearing values and methods. This is especially common for grandparents who were raised under the ethic of "spare the rod and spoil the child" or "children should be seen and not heard."

When it comes to a child's obedience, social and table manners, and training, today's times are very different from decades past. Today we use shunning and time-outs as forms of discipline, rather than spanking. Even the more loving and lenient grandparents find it hard to swallow the degree of permissiveness and fuzzy generational boundaries that can exist between some parents and children today.

Dotty, thirty-one, a single mother of three, has problems with her discipline-oriented dad. "He is a great guy, and it's a blessing to have him to help. And he wants to help. He is here after school every day for the kids. When I come home from work, we eat dinner together . . . but he is too harsh with them. He's like the Great Santini. The funny part is he has mellowed a bit in his old age, but he still is living in the past. He gets angry so easily and has such high standards. The kids are uptight around him. Of course, he never spanks them, like he did us, but he has very harsh reactions when the kids foul up. He gives them a little swipe when they do something wrong. My kids say his face gets red. I survived it, but I don't want him doing the same things he did to my kids that he did to me."

Her father, Pete, sixty-eight, feels that Dotty is too permissive with the children and that they walk all over her. "I've got to get them in shape. They have no manners and they eat like animals. Dot just throws food on the table, and they are like pigs at a trough. They take their plates and go to watch TV. All of us need to sit down together and eat like a family. And the way they talk to Dot. . . . I don't believe it. They have no idea how hard she works to keep it together. If I ever talked to my mother like that, I wouldn't have been able to sit down for a week."

It took Dotty and her dad over a year, with counseling, to settle their differences and build a consistent family team policy—one that valued Pete's commitment to help Dotty as a single parent and at the same time required that he follow Dotty's rules for raising her children. With respect, understanding, and flexibility, things changed for the better. Pete was especially happy when the children's table manners improved after Dotty agreed on having a "sit-down-together–no TV" meal every evening.

As parents, we set the rules for disciplining our child. It behooves us to make it clear to members of our family team how we want our child taught discipline, language, manners, respect, and more. The best way to do this is to convene a family conference, where we let our wishes be known and proceed to a respectful discussion.

Competition Between Grandparents

Favoritism works both ways. A child wants to be a favorite grandchild. So most grandparents want to be special—"the favorite"—to a grandchild. This leads to a natural competition between grandparents for the number one slot.

Whether a grandparent is favored or not depends on the number of available grandchildren and how close (emotionally and geographically) the grandparent is to a grandchild. The more grandchildren a grandparent has, the better the odds are to be favored by one. The more time they spend with their grandchild, the closer they are to the child and the less they may feel threatened or displaced by other grandparents.

For example, a grandparent living next door to a grandchild has the opportunity to be more involved than a grandparent who lives far away. When the "other" grandparents come to visit, the "next-door" grandparent can afford to be generous and allow the other grandparents time alone with the child. In this situation, any feelings of competition are diminished, even absent, because no competition exists. The next-door grandparent is number one.

This competitive grandparent urge may cause problems for parents. Teresa, twenty-four, has to deal with her mother-in-law, Crista, fifty-six, who is so "in love" with her grandson, Gabriel, two, that she doesn't want the other grandparents to "get their hands on him." That's because Crista doesn't like Gabriel's other grandparents.

"They are so different from us. I love Teresa, of course, but she is different from the rest of the family. They are so noisy. Teresa is more ladylike and has better taste."

Both Teresa and her husband, Luke, thirty, feel that Crista is "a bit of a snob." Luke said, "My mother is a great mother, but she is very picky. Teresa's parents are great: down-to-earth, the opposite of my mother. The funny part is that they think my mother is an uppity character—they call her 'Hyacinth,' like the woman in the English TV sitcom *Keeping Up Appearances*."

Luke and Teresa had to tell Crista to stop criticizing and competing with Teresa's parents. They said that it was hurting Teresa's parents' feelings and would eventually "put bad things" in Gabriel's mind about his other grandparents.

Crista said that she would try to bite her tongue, but it wouldn't be easy. Teresa asked Crista to refrain from criticizing her parents in front of her because she didn't feel the same way. Crista said, "I don't like it but I'll do it."

We need to be alert to competitive behavior between grandparents that originates from personality differences or controlling behavior. Be alert if grandparents want to be too close, vie to be the favorite side of the family, have a child adhere to their way of living or their values, or apply pressure in the form of guilt trips—for example, on where and when you spend the holidays. Some may pressure you too much to live close by and even offer to pick up the expenses for you to move where they are (although it is great to do when everyone is emotionally close and such an arrangement can be worked out). Although these desires on the part of grandparents are understandable, let them know if there is too much pressure attached to them. An alternative is to manage this zeal in a complimentary way by validating their need to be close and using their diversity, talents, and resources in the service of the family. For example, some parents get more financial support from one set of grandparents (who can afford it) than from the other.

Competing grandparents can adversely affect a child. If you are in such a situation, make sure to check out how your child feels. Does the child feel torn between the grandparents? Does the child play off one set of grandparents against the other? Does the child recognize being the "prize" in the competition between grandparents? Is the child being accorded undue authority by an adult who needs the child's approval for one reason or another?

The best treatment for grandparents who are competing for favored grandparent is humor. Identify the problem and mention it from time to time. Sue, thirty-four, says, "All of the grandparents are competing to be number one for my child. I keep a scorecard and let them all know where they are in the standings. Now we all laugh about it." When the lighthearted approach does not work, and the competition gets out of hand, it must be managed. If this is the case, make it known to grandparents that children who are the object of such a competition become insecure and inauthentic in their actions with their grandparents. What nature has created as unconditional love is distorted when grandchildren serve as the prize, the judge, and the jury in their grandparents' popularity contest. It's easy for children in this situation to become materialistic and to take advantage of the bounty offered them. Their love is no longer freely given but doled out according to how much their grandparents can do for them and buy for them. Such a situation becomes a travesty of a true vital connection.

The negative effects of grandparent competition can split couples apart. This happens when parents are sometimes forced to choose sides with their own parents against "the other side." Vanda, thirty-eight and the mother of five children, found that her parents and in-laws were in a "potlach" competition for the attention of the kids. "The cost of the presents escalated out of control. My dad bought my oldest son a motorbike, and my father-in-law bought him a car. It got to the point where my husband and I had to intervene and return the gifts. That didn't sit well with our son, who was having a ball."

Zach, her husband, thought, "It was funny. I saw the kids were benefiting and really didn't care. At first, I couldn't understand why Vanda was so off the walls about it. We had a couple of arguments, but when I saw it get out of control, we got on the same page."

Feuding Grandparents

When maternal and paternal grandparents are intolerant and disrespectful of one another's differences in culture, religion, race, socioeconomic status, and more, parents, caught in the middle of the fracas, can suffer. These types of conflicts threaten family solidarity. Unfortunately, they are becoming increasingly frequent, because society is becoming increasingly diverse. The chances that your children's grandparents (on the other side of the family) come from another culture or embrace religious beliefs that differ from your own are high today. It is not a surprise if they are not so accepting of one another's history, or attitudes. Although experiencing family diversity can be enriching for a child, grandparents may feel threatened.

When grandparents handle diversity in a mature manner, everyone wins. Mishandling the situation can have serious consequences. If you face such an issue, you will have to act as mediator. I get into this issue in detail in Chapter Nine. For now, here is a brief discussion of some differences that can breed conflicts.

1. *Ethnic-cultural differences*. When grandparents have different cultural backgrounds, it can lead to a lack of personal understanding, identity confusion, and cultural competition. Because legacy is of primal importance to grandparents, they may compete for one belief system or another to prevail and to pass on to the children. This is not easy for parents, who will be constantly pressured to choose one way or the other.

2. *Socioeconomic differences*. When one set of grandparents has more economic resources than the other, it can give rise to misunderstanding, competition, and resentment. Here's one example: Sheila, sixty-three years old, a single working grandmother, said of her counterparts, "My grandchildren's other grandparents are loaded with dough and are trying to buy the kids' love."

   If economic diversity exists between grandparents, it is mandatory for parents to equalize the playing field and set consistent financial guidelines for all to follow. Phyllis, a mother of two teenagers, understood early on that her in-laws were financially much better off than her widowed mother was. She quickly made it clear to her husband's parents that she has an "equitability policy" toward gift giving. She allows only three gifts per side at Christmas. "My in-laws are much better off financially than my mother, and I didn't want gift giving to get out of hand. I laid down some rules, and now the children know what to expect."

3. *Religious differences*. When grandparents are devoutly religious but adhere to a belief system that is different from a parent's beliefs, expect them to try to nudge the child to their way of

believing. As a parent, you have first "dibs" in promoting your own ideas and beliefs with your child. It is always good if you can include any of the grandparents' beliefs that are compatible with your own. In Chapter Nine, I explain why the best strategy is to look for as much common ground as possible and show how you can do it.

4. *Values and lifestyle differences.* Differences in personal values, politics, and lifestyles can raise strong passions that can pit grandparents against one another and leave you in the middle. Von, eighteen years old, put it well: "One of my grandfathers, Jim, who I love very much, is a tough kind of guy and often says things that are kind of racist. My other grandfather hates him, so we never invite them to the house together."

Von's parents have to deal with both of them. His mother says that the situation is driving her "nuts," for fear that they will both show up at the same time. In reaction, Von's father has arranged a visiting schedule so they don't meet up. "This takes a lot of time," says Von's mom.

5. *Bad personal chemistry.* For reasons unknown (that we may attribute to temperamental differences or "bad chemistry"), some grandparents just do not care (to say the least) for their grandchild's other grandparents. Rita, a fifty-five-year-old grandmother, said, "I just don't like my daughter-in-law's parents. They are loud, materialistic, and narrow-minded. Frankly, I would prefer that my granddaughter not be exposed to them or their ways. But there is not a damn thing I can do about it unless I want to start trouble in the family. I just have to live and let live. After all, my granddaughter is their granddaughter too."

Venus, thirty-six, her daughter-in-law, says, "The grandparents on both sides of this family just don't get along. It's such a strain on me. I have to be careful not to schedule anything where they will be alone with one another. You can cut the air with a knife for all the bad vibes. It's a real worry for me."

Because these grandparents feel righteous and have no wish to accommodate one another, all Venus can do to manage the situation is to keep them away from one another as much as possible. "We go to church as a family," she says. "One Sunday, we sit with my husband's parents; the next Sunday, we sit with my own parents. However, we all sit on the same side of the aisle so no one else knows what's goin' on."

Parents with four involved and supporting grandparents have a powerful support system. Parents with competing grandparents have, as one parent put it, "four more babies to deal with." Fortunately, we can harness the positive forces within competing grandparents for the good of the family.

What is necessary is for parents to maintain openness, forcefulness, and the ability to draw the line. Building a strong individual relationship with every grandparent is important. Standing your ground is important. Stopping any competition by banning presents over a certain amount of money, for example, might be a good, temporary way to make the point. Boycotting is a good strategy when carefully employed—for example, refusing to participate in an event where there is sure to be a spat or bad "vibes." What works best in overcoming these difficulties is striving to help the parties recognize their differences; affirm their commitment to the family, if not one another; listen attentively to the other's point of view; tolerate, honor, and respect the right of the person to that point of view; and negotiate differences quickly, before conflicts become more serious. But be prepared for disappointments. Sometimes the only benefit is that your child will admire you for trying.

Too Much Grandparenting

Conflicts occur even among people with the best of intentions. Too much grandparenting is an exaggeration of the normal interest and joy that grandparents take in their grandchildren. An example of this behavior is when loving, enthusiastic, and overjoyed grandparents want to be constantly—and obsessively—involved with their grand-child. Such zeal can stifle personal parent-child time, especially for those of us who don't have enough private time with our child.

Take, for example, Jordan, thirty-eight, who complained that his own parents, who lived nearby, were always "over at my place. Their interest is great, of course. However, I work all week and want some private time with my new son on the weekends. But my parents are always over at my house playing with him. They say they just cannot get enough of my son. They love him so much. I am going to have to talk with them about this, but I don't want to hurt their feelings." Fortunately, Jordan's direct approach worked. He worked out a schedule for the grandparents to visit that did not conflict with his own time with his child.

The emotional fallout from too much grandparenting is not as serious as a boundary conflict because these grandparents do not want to replace parents or usurp their place. It is also different from what can happen when grandparents care for children while parents work. In this situation, parents greatly appreciate the grand-parents' involvement.

Although too much grandparenting pleases most grandchildren, parents may feel overwhelmed by "too much of a good thing," as Velma, thirty-six, said, "I get invaded every day by my parents, and they are upset if I am not at home when they come. They even bring their friends to show them the baby. They do not think about me—my feelings and my privacy. But they are not doing anything bad, loving Juanita the way they do. They are good people, and telling them not to come over would hurt them. Normal visits would be fine. The only solution I can think of is moving away, but that's too radical, and I have my whole family here."

What Velma needs to do is to confront her parents directly (as Jordan did), air her feelings, and resolve the conflict. Velma is not demanding anything unreasonable, so if she addresses the issue with her parents in a noncritical way, they should get the message. Moving away is not a good solution. We must always strive to get rid of the problem, not the relatives.

Too Little Grandparenting

Today, more than ever, there are many grandparents who are unavailable for their grandchildren (and their own children as well). This is so common today that I have coined the term *grandorphan* to describe children in need of active and involved grandparents. There are many reasons this happens. Often both grandparents and parents are responsible for the separation.

Grandparents may not be available out of choice (they are disinterested) or unavailability (work, distance, illness, and so forth). Parents may reject grandparents' involvement because they dislike them (feuds) or ignore them because it is inconvenient due to distance or the logistics of getting the generations together. Sometimes well-meaning grandparents are not as available as they would like to be simply because they have too many grandchildren, and there are just not enough of them to go around. Whatever the reason, the family team is weakened with too little grandparenting.

Many grandparent-deprived parents complain that they need a substitute grandparent for their child. "I have a grandorphan," Zora, a twenty-six-year-old mother, lamented. "All my child's grandparents live far away. I am upset about it, yet I don't have the heart to ask any of them to move closer." Zora needs to make her needs known. As we will see in Chapter Ten, she might be very surprised that some of the grandparents may want to be as close to her as she wants to be to them.

The pain of grandparent deprivation is especially hurtful when there is an exceptional need for a grandparent's time, effort, or financial support—for example, with an adopted child, or a rebellious adolescent child testing the boundaries of his or her parents' love and commitment, or a youngster with special needs or a handicap.

This is the case with Al, seven, who was born blind and deaf. His divorced mother, Wendy, has to manage him alone. "Al was born blind and deaf. My parents cannot handle it at all. I can understand how they feel, but we need them. They brag about their other grandchildren and don't even talk about Al. There is so much they can do to help . . . but they don't."

In cases where grandparents are reticent about becoming involved, I have found it helpful to urge the grandparents to spend as much time as possible *alone* with their grandchild. Sometimes nature goes to work and allows love to break through and cement the bond. Where there's a will, there's a way. Cut off from her parents' help, Wendy was able to accomplish this with her retired ex-father-in-law, who was in recovery at Alcoholics Anonymous. He took Al under his wing and bolstered by the excellent ethics and values propounded by this great organization changed both their lives for the better.

I always suggest that parents tell grandparents exactly how they feel and exactly what they need. This resonates with the parent within the grandparent. Communicating in such a manner is usually successful, as long as the grandparent does not have a narcissistic personality disorder. As I will explain in detail in Chapter Eleven, more often than not, grandparents are willing to help when asked directly.

What about grandparents who just do not want to be bothered, or who are too busy, or who are too self-centered to participate on the family team? Or those who aren't available because they have moved miles away? Or those who may live near one child, but far away from any others? Often grandparent deprivation occurs because of lack of foresight on the part of family members. Conceiving of the family as a mutual team is the best way to prevent grandorphans. That is because the family team understands the importance of togetherness and strives to maintain it at all costs.

All we can do when grandparents resent or reject our requests to become part of the family team is to address the issue directly and let them know how needed and important they are. If a grandparent is relatively emotionally healthy, there is a good chance that such a plea can work. If a grandparent is self-centered or has another personality problem, it can fail, for the moment at least.

"Of course, I love my kids and the grandkids," said Achmad, a sixty-six-year-old grandfather, "but I just don't have the time to work and to spend all the time with them that my son and daughter-in-law want. When I am finished working, I like to relax and be with my friends, play cards, you know. It's part of my culture. I don't hang around with kids too much."

His daughter, Saroya, forty-six, was resigned to her children being grandparent deprived. "My children don't know their grandfather. I don't know him well either because he wasn't much of a father. I thought that being a grandfather, and having the children love him, would change him. But it didn't. He is still the same egotistical person he always was. He makes an appearance from time to time, but he is never involved. It's too bad because he is the only living grandparent my children have."

Achmad is the narcissistic exception to the rule that children are naturally attractive to grandparents and can actually induce grandparent behavior in reluctant grandparents. Over the years, I have advised grandparent-deprived parents to find a surrogate grandparent for their child from within the family (older aunts or uncles are great) or the community. Mentor programs and adopt-grandparent programs, which screen volunteers carefully, supply wonderful older friends for children. I have urged many parents who belong to a religious community to seek out older people to act as surrogate grandparents and form a support group for themselves as well. If you are seeking surrogate grandparents, see the Resources section for more information on how to start such a group.

Most of us have been affected by the way that changing times have altered the nature and structure of so many families. Keeping our family team together and well balanced in the face of these changes is a full-time job. We all need help to do so. In the next chapter, we'll discuss the complexities of family rearrangements and how they affect family members.

8

Family Rearrangements

We cannot take anything for granted nowadays. That is why one of the greatest challenges that we face today is to maintain and manage our family while so many changes are taking place, changes that have evolved beyond the traditional family to a variety of different family forms. Such changes are not only disorienting but also highly complicated. Divorce and remarriage, for example, blanket parents with layers upon layers of new people and circumstances to deal with. The possibilities for conflict that accompany such change are endless.

Some of the most common conflicts generated by structural family change are related to divorce, remarriage, "inherited (step) grandparents," and the repercussions of stepparenting. Change affects grandparents too. Parents need to know about two new and emerging phenomena—grandparent divorce and grandparent remarriage—that can upset and disorient both parents and grandchildren. Fortunately, there are basic principles and strategies that we may apply to help us deal with any of these situations.

Divorce

Divorce cracks the family team (two parents) at its center. When divorce occurs, each parent splits off from the original family team and starts anew as a single parent. As a result, each parent becomes the sole center of his or her own family team. Because divorce is so common today, many parents find themselves in such a situation, at least for a period of time. In fact, one out of three (first) marriages ends in separation or divorce during the first ten years, and 43 percent within fifteen years. Because one million children experience a divorce each year (50 percent of children before their eighteenth birthday), divorced parents need to maintain continuity for the child while minimizing any emotional damage. Parents also have to do the emotional work to accommodate to the divorce. This long and difficult process can create a hotbed of conflict that often touches all three generations.

Maintaining the child-grandparent connection can be hard for a parent while the flames of conflict burn hot during the divorce process (see Chapter Eleven, Asking for Emotional Support). After a divorce, one of the most difficult things that a parent has to do is to maintain a relationship with an ex-spouse's parents, as grandparents. Having to do this may be more of a problem for divorced mothers than fathers. That's because mothers usually have custody of children after divorce. In fact, research shows that contact with paternal grandparents may be decreased after a divorce—a situation rife with the possibilities of conflict.

If you are divorced, I cannot emphasize how important it is that in spite of how and what you feel toward your ex-partner and whether you are single, partnered, or officially remarried at the moment, you strive to keep your family team intact, if only for the sake of your children. That means dealing with former in-laws. This may not be easy, especially if there is strife between you. If you are unhappy in your marriage and are considering a divorce, you can limit the emotional fallout as far as grandparents are concerned. Line up any grandparents for help as soon as you feel any stirrings that your marriage may be ending. If you do not, you may encounter a great deal of unnecessary trouble. Here is why.

When a marriage is not going well, and hopes for healing are waning, it is natural for grandparents (and others, of course) to want to support their own child in the conflict. Usually, each partner's family of origin chooses to justify and support their child's position, although I have frequently seen exceptions to this. One common exception is when someone is blatantly at fault for the demise of the marriage (infidelity, drugs, crime, and the like), and that person's partner has an excellent relationship with the offending spouse's side of the family. Another exception is when someone's own parents are generally critical of their child and side with the partner in a conflict or divorce.

So unless you have a close relationship with your ex-partner's family, chances are, you will find yourself at odds with your in-laws over one issue or another. Any feud with them that results in your being alienated from them creates the loss of an important grandparent component of your family team. So unless there is a blatant reason to shun them, it is best to keep the connection viable, in one way or another, if only for your child's sake.

After the Divorce

A poor preexisting relationship with a grandparent is usually worsened by divorce. This is true for Russell, forty-three, who said that his own parents "never accepted anything I did. I could never do anything right for them. They told me I got married too young. They were against the marriage in the first place. I swear now they are gloating since I got divorced. They said they didn't like my wife in the first place. They told me so, they said. That's infuriating. I get nothing from them for me. If they were not close to my kids and help me care for them when I have them, I would not give them the time of day."

After the divorce, do not blame your in-laws too much if they pick sides and lose their objectivity about the situation. Most likely, you would do the same for your own child. The natural process of separation makes people devalue what they can't have or have to give up. This often makes us lose perspective. Understand, therefore, that it is natural for former in-laws to defend their child and even blame you for the divorce. It is equally natural for you to have negative feelings about them, especially if you were not too close in the first place. So don't be surprised if you have "positive" feelings about separating from them.

Dealing with former in-laws, however, should not be your first priority. You first need to work through your own feelings of sadness, disappointment, anger, and loss. This is where your own parents will come in handy. You must also shelter your child from the emotional fallout. It is essential that you handle your feelings toward your ex-partner and your partner's family in a constructive way that makes it as easy as possible for your child to relate to both sides of the family. When both partners are able to do this, the pain of the child is minimized.

When Crystal, forty-four, attended her son's high school graduation ceremony, she wanted to sit as far away as possible from her ex-husband and his new wife, who also attended, and from his parents. She was angry with her ex-husband for being consistently late on his child support payments and negligent in fathering their three children. Crystal's two other children were torn about whom to sit with, as each of their parents, and grandparents, were sitting on opposite sides of the auditorium. Sensing her children's discomfort, Crystal did a wonderful thing. She got up from her seat and reseated herself, her parents, and the children as close as possible to the stage. Then she beckoned to her ex-husband, his wife, and his parents to come and join her. She seated the two children between them so, in her words, "My son could see his whole family when he was up on the stage getting his diploma." Crystal put her child's feelings above her own. That's selflessness.

Understand that your child most likely will not have the same feeling about your former in-laws that you do, especially if the child is close to those grandparents. You may want to discontinue your relationship, but your child can't, because they are his grandparents. Therefore, like Crystal, you may have to swallow your feelings, bite your tongue, and do the best you can when you are asked to keep your child in contact with them. There is a good reason to make such an effort.

Maintaining the Family Team

In-laws can become ex-in-laws, but as grandparents, they remain the same for the child. When children are in the picture, a divorced parent is stuck with the in-laws. If a parent is close to them personally, all the better. That makes keeping the family team together much easier. When a parent isn't close and desires to cut any close personal ties, it will upset the child. That's because the child views the same people as part of the other parent's family team. This makes the child happy, contributes to the idea that the child has two families who love him, and thereby limits the losses that result from the divorce.

Anything that is good for the child is good for the parent as well. Dealing with the "other side" in a divorce can be difficult to do. The potential for conflict and complications is limited only by the nature, quality, and circumstances of the former relationships. The heat of the battle depends on the amount of residual anger that remains between the divorced parties, how close they remain emotionally, whether the decision to divorce was mutual, whether anyone feels victimized, the amount of geographical distance, and other factors too numerous to mention.

Because of all these factors, keeping a child and former in-laws together may be one of the most difficult things a parent ever has to do. For example, Myra, thirty-eight, always "acts polite" with her ex-in-laws, although she dislikes them. After her contentious divorce, she sought therapy because she was becoming depressed. Her own parents lived far away and were therefore not available to help her on a permanent basis. Although her former in-laws lived in the same town, she wanted nothing to do with them.

"I don't want to see them anymore," she said, "but I have no choice. I am stuck with them because of my children. My children love them. It is such a burden on me to arrange visits. Either I have to drive my children to their house and pick them up, or they come over when I have better things to do. I don't know why they cannot see the children when my ex-husband takes them. They always want more. We are always fighting about when, where, and what time they want to see the children. Sometimes I think I can't take it anymore. I am trying to find a way to cut down on their visits, but I know my children will object."

In therapy, Myra carefully analyzed her feelings and the complex issues involved. She began to work through her own feelings of anger and resentment about the divorce (her husband had had an affair). After a lot of hard work, she began to see the value of her in-laws for her child. She also had to unhook them emotionally from the anger she felt toward her ex-husband. Eventually, she was able to sit down with her in-laws, express her feelings, let them know she honored their relationship with the children, and arrange a sensible schedule. By so doing, she reconstituted her family team and now uses her appreciative in-laws as a resource to help her with the children when she needs it. She also makes a concerted effort to keep any negative feelings about the in-laws from her children, which they also greatly appreciate.

"It was all worth the effort," she said. "Not only did it make me grow up; what I did took a great deal of pressure off of the children, when I stopped burdening them with my feelings." Some of the thoughts and attitudes that Myra used to work through her feelings and reconstitute her family team can be useful for any parent involved in a divorce issue.

Guidelines and Principles for Maintaining the Family Team After Divorce

Keeping in mind the following principles will aid you in maintaining an effective family team, which is in your child's best interest.

- Although I am divorced, my child is not. My ex-spouse's parents, my child's grandparents, are permanently present in his psyche. They are therefore part of my life whether I like it or not.
- My child's feelings are different from my own.
- I will try to acknowledge, evaluate, and work through my own feelings about the divorce.

- I will try to listen to the feelings of others about my divorce.

- I will be compassionate, understanding, loving, and supportive of my child's relationships with all grandparents.

- I will call an occasional meeting with my former in-laws to assess our needs and modify our plan to continue the grandparent-grandchild relationship.

- I will shelter and support my child through this painful process. My child will benefit from observing my efforts to keep our family team intact, traumatized as it may be.

- I will seek support from friends and family and activate my own parents as much as possible to fill any breach in my family team.

- I will always keep in mind that the effects of divorce are life-long because, through our child, I will always be connected as a co-parent to my former spouse. I recognize that the degree of anger between us is proportional to how much the children suffer.

- I know I can't do everything I would like to do all of the time, so I will be kind and forgiving toward myself.

- Doing all this makes me a better and stronger person.

Remarriage and Inherited Grandparents

The majority of divorced persons remarry and create stepparents and inherited stepgrandparents. In the United States, the high divorce and subsequent remarriage rate has created tens of millions of stepparents and stepgrandparents. In fact, the Stepfamily Association of America estimates that more than two-thirds of all women—more than half of all Americans—and one-third of all children will spend some time in a stepfamily (accounting for remarriage and cohabitation). When an individual gets together with a partner with children, the child's grandparents are included in the family package. When a parent brings a child to a new marriage, the child inherits their new stepsiblings' biological grandparents as stepgrandparents.

The child's own grandparents become stepgrandparents to the new stepsiblings as well. The addition of so many folks to the family team, like so many other situations, can be a blessing or a curse. It all depends on the how the situation is handled.

If you are a stepparent, making the necessary emotional and logistical adjustments to stepparenthood will require a great deal of self-examination and maturity. Unless you were lucky enough to have had a good stepparent when you were a child, you are probably unfamiliar with how one acts in the "step" role. Fortunately, there is a list of helpful organizations that you will find in the Resource section, which can offer helpful advice on how to be an effective stepparent. For now, I will focus on the daunting subject of dealing with inherited grandparents.

Dealing with a Can of Worms

Selma, forty-three, came for a consultation after she married Shed, forty-five. "I need help," she said. "My family is like a can of worms." Selma is in her third marriage. She has two children from her first marriage, which ended in divorce. She also has one child from her second marriage (she was widowed), and she now has two stepchildren from her marriage with Shed. Tallying up the family count, Selma's three children have six living biological grandparents (from Selma's parents and from her first and second husbands' parents). The children, now stepsiblings to Shed's children, also have two stepgrandparents. And there is more: Selma's parents are now stepgrandparents to Shed's children, and so on and so on. You get the picture.

Her glass is both half full and half empty. The possibilities for having a broad and deep family team are exciting. Conversely, keeping it all together can be exhausting. Add to the mix any residual resentment from divorce, coupled with personality and logistical problems, and it is not hard to understand how easily the family could come apart.

For example, the fact that Selma's parents were not treating all of the children equally (favoring their own grandchildren) caused quite a conflict between Selma and Shed. To quiet the waters, Selma called several meetings with her parents to let them know that they had to treat their stepgrandchildren and their biological grandchildren as equally as possible. She understood that they wanted to be alone with their grandchildren, and at first they were not interested in relating to Shed's children. As kind and considerate people, they listened carefully and did their best to comply with Selma's wishes. After a while, they began to enjoy Shed's children, and vice versa. Because Selma's parents were nice to his children, Shed has grown closer to them. Now Selma's only problem is logistical: keeping a schedule for her children and stepchildren to get together with all six grandparents.

Self-Examination for Remarriage and Stepparenting

Recognize that you have to understand your situation and that you need to get in touch with how you feel about taking on this new role. You will need to spend some quiet time alone and reflect on the following questions, especially as they relate to connecting your children with their biological grandparents as well as their stepgrandparents.

- Do I want or need this role?
- Am I enthusiastic about its possibilities, or do I see it as just another obligation, even a burden (especially with all the grandparents involved)?
- Do I have the time and desire to maintain a lifelong relationship with my stepchildren and their grandparents?
- Do I like my stepchildren's grandparents? Do they bring value to my family team?
- Are there family issues that may prevent me from establishing a good relationship with my stepchildren?
- What is my husband's attitude toward my involvement with his child and his child's grandparents?

- Are my husband and I in agreement about the type of relation-ship that we want to have with these new family members?

- Do I feel good about myself for trying to make it all work?

Dealing with Stepgrandparents

If you are a stepparent, the outcome of your efforts to relate to the grandparents of your stepchild is not totally in your hands. First, the degree of closeness that you achieve with your stepchild and the child's grandparents depends on their receptivity to a relationship with you. That can take time. What is under your control, however, is your ability to manage your own expectations and actions.

So when a stepchild and the child's grandparents come into your family, take a step back to carefully examine the situation as objectively as possible. Consider how emotionally close they were before you came into the family picture. The closer they are, the more you will have to deal with old habits. You will therefore want to proceed slowly. As Brad, a forty-one-year-old father of two and stepfather of three children, noted, "It took me over two years to be accepted by my new in-laws and for my stepchildren and their grandparents to accept me in a father role."

The circumstances leading up to a remarriage can seriously affect your relationship with stepgrandparents. Widowhood rarely causes a problem because there is no competition, except with the memory of the passed loved one. Usually, most of us honor and respect such tender emotions and give them a wide berth. When a parent dies, a new stepparent can be a welcome addition to the fam-ily. This may not be so in divorce. The more a divorce is con-tentious, the more rough the going for all generations.

For example, Kylie, twenty-three, feels that when she married her divorced husband, her two stepchildren's grandparents wanted nothing to do with her. "The children's mother told all of the grandparents that I broke up her marriage. Although my husband says that is not true and that he wanted to get divorced before he met me, they do not believe him. It came to the point where he said he was going to move away and leave all of them unless they accepted me. I guess things have improved in the last year, especially with my husband's father. We seem to get along well, but there is an edge. They liked my husband's first wife, and they don't want to let her go. I'm willing to wait." In spite of difficult circumstances, Kylie, with a positive attitude, is beginning to assemble, in a rudimentary way, the three dimensions of her family team, with her stepchildren on one side and her husband's father on the other.

The age of your stepchild is very significant. The younger your stepchild is, the easier it will be to forge a relationship, especially if you are a custodial stepparent. A baby is the best. A baby is ignorant of any negative family dynamics and is at a developmental stage where she will welcome all who adore her. With an older child, you have to reflect on her personality, experience, family issues, and her developmental state. A five-year-old will relate to you much more easily than a teenager, who is certainly preoccupied (if not obsessed) with school, friends, and activities. It is important to talk with the stepgrandparents about their expectations, how often they want contact with their grandchild, and so forth. When everyone pitches in, things can work well.

Give Stepgrandparents a Chance

As a stepparent, you become quickly aware of your stepchild's psychological state (because of the effects of the divorce and the process of bonding with you). Although it may not be immediately evident, grandparents go through an adjustment period as well. So make an effort to be considerate of what the grandparent is experiencing. Both children and grandparents in step situations have to deal with similar and profound psychological issues, including the following:

- Grieving and emotionally processing a parent's death or divorce
- Accepting the remarriage of a parent and then accepting a new stepparent

- Dealing with divided loyalties (to the previous family) because of remarriage
- Adapting to a family configuration of new siblings, aunts, uncles, and stepgrandparents

These powerful psychological processes can affect the new stepchild and grandparents so deeply that their emotional reserves are exhausted. Therefore, at first, there may not be much left over for you. So don't expect too much at the beginning. It is going to take time and effort to become closer.

This is what happened to Byron, a thirty-eight-year-old father of three. "My first wife died of breast cancer. Her parents died young, and my mother was my child's only living grandparent. When I remarried my wife Blema, who was never married before, my new in-laws, who are active, fun people, checked me out for two years. Then one day, they told me that they wanted to be real grandparents to my kids. I was very touched, because up to that point, my kids only had my mother, and she is not well. They asked me if that was OK and I said sure. Now they take the kids everywhere, go to their school plays, to the park, even biking! It is great too, because Blema and I get time alone together, which is a treat. In addition, the kids just love them. Now they are all taking tennis lessons together."

Balancing Grandparents

Here is another tricky aspect of the step situation. Some stepfamily teams can be overloaded on the grandparent side. If you are like Selma (whom I mentioned previously), whose children and stepchildren have six grandparents, it is going to be difficult to do your part to tend to their vital connections. If some of them do not get along, it is going to make things worse.

You too might have to face a situation where too many grand-parents compete for their grandchild's time and attention. If this occurs, you will have to take charge, being a mediator at one time and a dictator at another. If your stepchild has a previous close relationship with grandparents, it pays to nurture that bond at the same time that you forge one for yourself. Some grandparents might even feel envious of a stepparent's contact with their grandchild if they themselves are deprived of this contact.

If this is the case, it is important for the stepparent to discuss this issue with the grandparents. Grandparents need to hear that they are personally respected and that efforts will be made to get them together with their grandchild, especially if their child died and their grandchild's remaining parent remarried. They are going to be frightened of losing their grandchildren as well and will need reassurance. So set an example by making an effort to coordinate visits and coordinate gift giving during the holiday season. Stepparents must show that they respect the grandparents' relationship with their grandchild and want to enhance, not detract, from their loving bond.

Your Partner Counts

What effects one person in a couple affects the other as well. For this reason, your feelings toward your stepchild's grandparents will affect your partner, and vice versa.

For example, if your partner is feuding with a parent or an ex-in-law, chances are, you are going to be caught in the cross fire. If there is turmoil present, it is going to be difficult for you to become close to the family. If your partner is someone who is removed from family, chances are, he or she will want you to be as well. Whether you agree or not with your partner's ideas or attitudes toward one family member or another, it is important to get on the same page by hammering out a common policy that you can both agree on.

New stepparents may feel excluded initially by grandparents. That is what happened to Eunice, thirty-four, who sought consultation because she was becoming disheartened about her marriage. At the time that Eunice married Manfred, forty-five, he had joint custody of three young children by a previous marriage and was estranged from his parents. The rift occurred when Manfred had a business disagreement with his father and walked out of the bakery that they owned jointly. Although he no longer spoke with his father, Manfred allowed his parents to visit his children from time to time. Eunice, a kindergarten teacher, who loves children, was upset because the grandparents did not relate to her. She was convinced that it was because they were angry with Manfred, because they hardly knew her.

The grandparents did visit with the children when they were at their mother's house (Manfred's ex-wife) and were on good terms with her. Eunice had no living parents and wanted to have a closer relationship with Manfred's parents, especially after she became pregnant. While in therapy, she decided to make an effort to get closer to Manfred's parents and "nag" Manfred to "grow up and make up with his dad." By clever, slow maneuvering (inviting Manfred's parents for holiday dinners, going to their church, getting some "extra" theater tickets and inviting them), she finessed a family reconciliation. Now her child has "real" grandparents, and her stepchildren are fond of her. Manfred is grateful and she has a family team. As a bonus for her efforts, she has become friendly with Manfred's ex-wife, who has remarried. All this togetherness makes the children happy.

If you find yourself in this kind of situation, make an effort, like Eunice, to understand the dynamics of your stepfamily. Be aware of your own feelings and attitudes first, and then do the same for everyone else. You will find that in most cases, with love and patience, there will be room for you as a loving friend in your stepchild's life. You will also have a greater possibility of creating a family team with the child's grandparents. Here are some of the questions that Eunice asked herself and the principles that she applied during her effort to improve her situation:

- Examine your thoughts and feelings about how you can build a family team as a stepparent. What are your own expectations, dreams, wishes, and needs? How much energy do you want to put into this role? What are the returns for you? What

are the returns for others in your family? How does your partner feel about your getting involved in the first place? Who is
on the potential roster?

- Educate yourself about stepfamilies and stepgrandparenting.
  Learn all you can about how stepfamilies work. Observe other
  stepfamilies in operation. Learn from their successes and from
  their mistakes. (See Resources for educational material and
  networking organizations.)

- Assess your new family, and plan how you can construct your
  family team from the personnel available to you. Put yourself
  in everyone else's shoes. Ask your new family members individually how you can enhance the family system. Let them
  know you acknowledge, understand, and respect what they
  are going through.

- Observe your own feelings and thoughts about your new family situation and the people involved. Separate your own
  biases and preconceived ideas from the reality of the situation.
  Remain nonjudgmental.

- Watch and wait. At first, stay calmly at the periphery of the
  family system. Let things settle down. Be an available presence. Remember that children have a difficult time after a
  death, divorce, or remarriage and are trying to make sense of
  their new family configuration.

- Be a source of peace and pleasure. Stay in a positive role. Be
  close and available to those who reach out or need you. Stay
  at a loving distance from those who are negative, but try not
  to react to or perpetuate their negativity.

- Confront challenges and use them to grow. Set positive examples for the whole family to follow.

The role of stepparent is part art, part learning, part perseverance,
part commitment, and all love. It is an adventure too. If you are lucky,
you will have more than enough players to form your family team.

Alternatively, with skill, you can substitute step relationships for family regulars. Many people I know have created wonderful families by their efforts.

When Grandparents Divorce

As longevity is increasing, grandparent divorce is becoming more common. Like parental divorce, grandparent divorce rocks the foundations of the family, affecting all three generations of family members. Youngsters, who look up to their grandparents as stable and unchanging people, have to deal with their own reactions as well as the reactions of their parents. For parents, it is no easy task to have to deal with their own feelings about divorced parents, support each parent, and help their child as well.

Explaining grandparents' divorce to a child can be an especially difficult and complex undertaking. Over the years, I have learned that when a grandparent divorces, a child undergoes a modified version of the same thoughts and feelings experienced when a parent divorces. What is different, however, is dealing with its effect on the child's image of grandparents, as well as the child's concepts of family continuity, traditions, and place (whether it is the grandparents' traditional home or geographical location). It is up to the parent to understand this process and to help the child understand and digest this change in the family system.

When grandparents divorce, children's feelings range from confusion and emotional upset, if the grandparents are very close, to less intense emotions if the grandparents are distant. Feelings can also vary according to the degree of acrimony involved in the divorce. The more animosity, the more the child is upset. Children may have more concerns about one grandparent than the other depending on their closeness and how vulnerable they perceive the grandparent to be.

"When my grandparents divorced, I was fifteen," said Maude, now thirty-five years old. "I always felt worse for my grandmother because I knew her better than my grandfather. He was never around because he traveled so much. He just up and left her and she was devastated. There she was, an abandoned woman who had to support herself. She had given him the best years of her life. Grandpa still calls me and I love him, but I guess I am still very angry with him. I've tried all this time to get over it, but I don't know if I ever will. Mom isn't doing too well in forgiving him either."

Because many of the roles that grandparents play for children relate to stability and continuity, divorce brings sadness and disappointment as well as family disorientation. Siobhan, eighteen years old, said she grieved for one year when she learned about her grandparents' divorce.

"I knew they fought a lot, but I would never have thought they didn't love each other any more. I am so sad about it because they rather represent the family. Now, I can't explain it, I feel lost. My world is topsy-turvy. The whole family is sad about grandma and grandpa. We don't know what to do about holidays, who to invite. It is like all of the things we did every year stopped. You would think they were too old to want to get divorced. I looked up to them."

The deep disorientation of the child often is translated into a sense of family insecurity—especially if the parents are divorced too. Rolf, eight years old, was concerned about Thanksgiving without his grandfather.

"The whole family always spent Thanksgiving and Christmas together. It's true that grandpa did get drunk, and that's why grandma didn't want to be married to him anymore, but he never hurt us. He was silly when he drank. Now he won't be at grandma's for the holidays anymore. I am sick about what happened. I hope this doesn't happen to my parents. I always thought that my parents and grandparents would always be together. Now I worry about my parents getting divorced too. Can I count on any adults to stay together?"

Dealing with the Impact

The insecurity that the child experiences when grandparents divorce leads to an increased need for stability and security from their parents. They need to know how and why this happened and what they can count on. That's where parents need to mediate with grandparents on the child's behalf.

John, a sixty-two-year-old grandfather, told his son Will, thirty-eight, that he wanted to divorce Will's mother. With Will's permission, John talked with his two grandchildren and explained to them exactly what was going on. His granddaughter, Moira, eight years old, said, "I was happy my grandfather talked to us kids and told us that he still loved all of us. He said he and grandma did not want to be married anymore, but they still liked each other. He asked us to tell him how we felt, and we told him we were sad, and everyone started crying, even grandpa. He told us to call him to talk anytime. But I feel scared about marriage. If my grandparents get divorced, what does that say about getting married? Will this happen to me?"

It is often difficult for parents to explain to children why their grandparents act differently after they divorce. Geri, eleven years old, attended a birthday party of her divorced grandfather's girlfriend's granddaughter. Geri was upset when she saw her grandfather being affectionate with his girlfriend. "Yuck!" said Geri to her parents. "My grandfather was kissing that lady." Parental explanations, rationalizations, and lectures gushed forth.

Children want to maintain a relationship with both grandparents in a divorce and do not want to choose sides. Parents have to help. Stan, thirteen years old, and his grandfather are very close. He was very upset when his grandparents became divorced and his grandfather moved out. Stan told his grandmother that he was angry with his grandfather for divorcing her and marrying a much younger woman. His grandmother recognized Stan's sadness and his confusion about how to deal with the grandfather he loved. Instead of criticizing his grandfather and after talking the situation over with Stan's parents, his grandmother, in a most considerate and loving way, told Stan that the grown-ups' problems were not his problems. His parents reinforced the idea that his grandfather loved him and that what had happened was between both grandparents and had nothing to do with him. His grandmother's words were comforting to Stan, who, like most grandchildren, was concerned about protecting his grandmother because he viewed her as the most vulnerable of his grandparents.

It is important to help a child understand the reasons for the divorce (age appropriately, of course). Parents should also be aware that their child wants to protect them as well from feeling bad. Arnold, ten years old, said he felt sick when he heard that his grandparents were divorcing. "My parents got really angry and upset and started yelling at my grandparents. They were so upset I could not say how I felt because I felt sorry for my parents. They said they were ashamed. But my grandparents explained to them why they were getting a divorce. They said they wanted to get a divorce for a long time but wanted to wait until the children grew up. They made my parents feel better, and that made me feel better because I was feeling bad myself and didn't want to worry about my parents being so upset too." Older children can understand that people grow out of love or grow away from each other over the years. They can accept the fact that their grandparents have had a good life together until a certain point, that they still care for and respect each other, but that they now have decided to move on. This explanation keeps sacred what might be a great memory for a child.

When grandparents divorce, the most important thing that you can do for a child is to make yourself available to listen to his thoughts and feelings about the situation. Of course, only time heals such deep wounds. But being available to share a child's pain and confusion and to act as a sounding board helps decrease the destructive effects of the divorce.

Dominique, fifteen years old, said, "My mom helped me a lot when my grandparents got divorced. I wasn't used to seeing them without each other. However, whenever I called them, they responded. Both of them would drop whatever they were doing to see me. In addition, my mom would always bring me over to see one of them when I missed them or felt sorry for them, especially my grandma. They both remarried; they even have stepgrandchildren but are always still there for me when I need them. This was so important for me because they told me that things wouldn't change between us after they got divorced, and then they showed me they meant what they said."

Here are some guidelines to follow to minimize the effect of a grandparent's divorce on you and your child:

- Understand that a grandparent divorce has severe repercussions for all family members, especially grandchildren.

- First evaluate, acknowledge, and work through your own feelings about the divorce situation.

- Ask your children about their thoughts and feelings concerning the divorce.

- Try to insulate young children from adults' opinions and perceptions.

- No matter what you feel, do not ask children to choose sides in the divorce.

- Initiate your healing plan. Let family members know the facts of the divorce, and listen to their thoughts and feelings. Let children know only what is appropriate.

- Respect the grieving process and the confusion of your children.

- Set an excellent example. Be respectful of and do not interfere with family members' relationships with the divorced grandparents.

- Take care of yourself during this difficult time. Seek a friendly ear or even professional help if necessary. It is important for your family to see you working hard to make the best of a painful situation and striving toward healing. Include them in all aspects of this process.

Children easily absorb their parents' misery, so the better you cope with the situation, the better your children will cope. If you allow your family to share in the healing process, everyone will heal more quickly and will move on. Although a grandparent divorce has many painful aspects, there is sometimes an unseen benefit. Grandparents who remarry can expand the amount of people on the family team through step relationships.

When Grandparents Remarry

Much of what I explained earlier in the chapter about step relationships also applies to a grandparent's remarriage. You and your child will have to adjust to the new stepgrandparents on your family team and will have to deal with the feelings of your other parent. The principles I outlined in regard to step relationships can be applied in this case as well.

Accepting and accommodating diversity in intermarriage, race, religion, sexual orientation, and more is one of the greatest challenges we face. As we will see in the next chapter, such pronounced differences in the nature of the family in only one generation can breed serious conflicts between parents and grandparents.

9

Family Diversity

As we become an increasingly diverse nation, we are being continually challenged to reexamine our basic ideas, attitudes, and values. Many of us in the parent generation accept and readily accommodate to these changes. We were brought up with what our own parents consider to be radical change as the norm. Today's grandparents were brought up with more conventional and consistent habits and attitudes for a long period of their lives, before they began to encounter change. The pace of change was so rapid that their world went topsy-turvy in only one generation. Recent immigrants have had a similar experience. Rooted in the old ways, they have had to make a major adjustment to American attitudes and values.

Among the most radical changes is the positive shift away from sexist attitudes. Another is the increase in interracial marriages, almost unheard of until the latter part of the last century. In the year 2000, the Census Bureau reported seven hundred thousand Asian-white couples as well as four hundred thousand black-white couples. There are nearly two million couples in which one partner is Hispanic, and the other is from a different group. More than 50 percent of teenagers date interracially. Things are changing, and fast!

As we would expect, conflicts occur when new and old ideas and attitudes knock heads. Bad as it is when people have different political views, it is a lot worse when the opposing views and opinions concern family structure, values and attitudes, sexual behavior, religious differences, and intermarriage. And this is especially so when it comes to confronting old taboos concerning racial, ethnic, and religious differences and culturally embedded prejudices and boundaries.

It is therefore not hard to understand that such changes in personal family attitudes, tolerance, racist and sexist values, and more, occurring in only one generation, may stress even the most "evolved" person. This leads to conflict unless family members are tolerant of one another's views and assume a kind, understanding, noncritical, and nonjudgmental attitude.

In this chapter, we'll consider some of the most important issues that I have encountered between parents and grandparents that generate family conflicts. They are ethnic, racial, and religious differences and homosexual parenthood and grandparent issues. I will also address how a "straight" parent can deal effectively with a gay or lesbian grandparent.

Chances are, if you have not encountered the effects of diversity yet, you certainly will in the future. Your child is growing up in a world that will be increasingly more diverse than it is today. Diversity can enrich a healthy family team. However, if prejudices and intolerance prevail, the aftershocks can tear a family apart. The conflicts generated by diversity are as varied as the people involved. Racial, religious, and ethnic differences, for example, can be especially tough issues for parents and grandparents to address.

Fortunately, the method for dealing with diversity is similar in most situations. I'll use the issue of religious differences as an example to offer suggestions for helping and healing that may be applied to other diversity issues. By developing the understanding, along with these skills, you will be able to cope effectively with the effects of the inevitable changes brought about by diversity that you and your child will face in the coming years.

Religious Concerns

Religious differences between people have been a cause for conflict and even wholesale slaughter throughout human history. Although this clash most often takes place on a tribal or national level, individual families are not spared. In the recent past (and still in some Third World countries today), elders chose marriage partners for their young, based on an ethnic, regional, and religious "match." Not so in the western melting pot, where we experience an increase in religious, ethnic, and racial "mismatches" due to extensive intermarriage. This can lead to lots of conflicts, but, it is hoped, not wholesale slaughter.

What concerns many grandparents in religious matters is the continuity of religious beliefs from one generation to the other. Because most of today's grandparents remain loyal to the beliefs they were born with, it is natural for them to want to inculcate their children and grandchildren in the same "ancestral" way. Conflict can arise, however, when today's parents do not want to follow their ancestral path. Discontinuity in beliefs can result when parents partner with someone of a different persuasion and change their beliefs. Or it can occur when parents choose to have different beliefs from their own parents and raise their children differently from their grandparents. Some parents claim not to have any beliefs at all.

Nevertheless, shared beliefs bring people together. So it is understandable that most parents would prefer that their children follow in their beliefs, worshipping together, sharing holidays. When they notch up one generation, into parents and grandparents, the more "believing" the grandparents are, the more they prefer that their children identify with their belief system. When parents don't conform, animosity can occur. When grandchildren come along, the situation can get worse.

The more entrenched the grandparents' beliefs are, the more they are going to want their grandchildren to become acquainted with—if not adhere to—their beliefs. This is especially so because the transmission of religious beliefs is part of the *spiritual guide* function of grandparents. Part of this role involves the urge of grandparents to pass their own beliefs to their children, and especially to their grandchildren. In fact, research shows a positive link for grandparents between their degree of family involvement and their own religiosity.

As one researcher noted, "Religious grandparents are generally more greatly involved in family and social ties."[1] Simply put, it is important for parents to understand that religion, and the transmission of religious beliefs, can be very important issues for grandparents. When parents have different beliefs, it can lead to lots of conflicts.

The Impact of Parents on a Separate Path

When parents decide to tread a different religious path from their forebears, their own parents often feel confused, disappointed, deeply saddened, and often angry, because of the loss of religious continuity in the family. The more adamant the parties are about adhering to their different beliefs, the greater the emotional fireworks.

Winton, twenty-six, has parents who are pillars of her local church. Big trouble started when she married Tim, twenty-six, an outspoken agnostic. "My parents are furious at me for marrying Tim. He does not want our children to attend church and be 'brainwashed,' as he says. My parents' life is their church, and they are beside themselves with anger. I do not care one way or the other. I just want peace. Of course, the kids would rather sleep in on Sunday morning rather than go to church. But they do like the 'fun' part of church, getting shown off by my parents. My parents' attitude has created a rift with Tim, and I am caught in the middle."

After Winton was "fed up" with the turmoil in her family, she called a family meeting with Tim and her parents. She told everyone that she found their feuding intolerable. After a long discussion, a compromise was reached. The grandparents could take the children to church once a month but had to promise not to "brainwash" them.

"If the kids want to go to church when they are eighteen, it's up to them," said Tim. "Right now, *my* views have to be respected too. But I am willing to compromise for peace."

His father-in-law said, "That's very Christian of Tim."

Religious conflicts between adults have an effect on children too. Michael, forty-six, reported that during the early years of his marriage, his "very orthodox" (Eastern Rite) parents kept their distance from

Alex, Michael's daughter, because his parents disapproved of his raising his children in his wife's Episcopalian religion.

"Alex is being brought up as an Episcopalian because my wife cares so much about it. My father finds it hard to get close to Alex because she has a different religion, and he does not want to step on my wife's toes or confuse Alex. Therefore he withdraws. Alex likes her grandfather and feels that he does not want to spend time with her."

"He acts weird," she said at the time.

Michael's father said that his religion was the center of his life and that he wanted to teach his granddaughter about it and worship with her. "I feel disconnected to her; she has a different religion and way of thinking about it. It's a big obstacle."

Fortunately, when Alex was seven, and with some guidance, Michael confronted the issue and discussed the conflict openly and objectively with his wife and parents separately. As a result, Michael and his wife agreed to let Alex attend her grandfather's church and to learn about his religion from an "educational" point of view. "Now Alex and my dad are like peas in a pod," smiled Michael.

Like Michael, I agree that we should try to be tolerant and respectful of grandparents' beliefs and allow our child to learn about and participate in their ethnic or religious practices. At the least, it is a learning experience for the child. Diversity itself should not be viewed as a threat. Exposure to diverse ideas, attitudes, behaviors, and ways should be viewed as a part of the child's spiritual education. Love, understanding, acceptance, and tolerance are the watchwords. We should, however, make it clear to grandparents not to criticize our beliefs or proselytize their own to our child. With this caution, everyone wins.

Here is an example of how parents can successfully address such issues: "I am a Catholic," said Deb, a sixty-two-year-old grandmother of four. "My daughter, Noreen, has chosen to raise her child with no religious education at all. I really do not approve of that. I think my grandchildren need to be brought up with Christian values, especially in today's world. Her choice has hurt our relationship. I feel disconnected in some way from my child and grandchildren."

Noreen, forty-five, is sad about the possibility of being alienated from her mother. "My mother has the right to her beliefs," she said, "but I don't believe in her religion for a lot of reasons, some personal, others intellectual. I am not going to expose my kids to what I consider a limited view of spiritual life. My mother has to understand this. Having different religions doesn't mean we can't be close. If she wants to make us miserable over this, it's her problem."

Fortunately, after a lot of soul-searching and consultation with her spiritual adviser, Deb was able to accept Noreen's viewpoint and felt happy when she was allowed to take her grandchildren to church on Christmas. Her daughter chalked this up to "part of their education, and making my mother happy." Tolerance, understanding, and flexibility work.

Challenging Ethnic and Cultural Tradition

Passing on family history and cultural values is the stuff of grandparenting. That is why differences that challenge deeply rooted religious, ethnic, racial, and cultural family traditions at the same time can be especially difficult.

Mordecai is a seventy-nine-year-old Jewish grandfather who escaped from a concentration camp in Poland during the Holocaust. The rest of his family was killed. Mordecai's religion, like Deb's, is very important to him, as well as his Jewish culture, which involves language and rituals. His son, Sam, thirty-eight, married Chantal, twenty-five and a Catholic, four years ago. They have one three-year-old daughter. Sam agreed to raise her as a Catholic when he married Chantal in the Catholic Church.

"I am an American," Sam told me. "I don't want to be Jewish because it means nothing to me. Of course, if the SS ever comes around, I will be Jewish again, but that is about all the connection I feel to the religion. If it means a lot for Chantal to raise her child as a Catholic, that is OK. When we got married in the church, I promised that. It's fine with me as long as I don't have to be involved. If Chantal is happy, I am happy. My work as a professor of astronomy is my religion."

Meanwhile, however, Mordecai is distraught about his grandchild losing her Jewish identity and heritage. "Judaism is my world. Since time began, my people have been persecuted, but we are still on the earth. Why? Because of our religion and our sticking together. Now I can't pass on this heritage to my darling granddaughter because her mother won't let her be Jewish. Now my family's religious traditions, what so many died for, are going to be erased. What do I do? I never considered that I would not have Jewish grandchildren. I am glad my wife never lived to see this."

A similar example is Thanh, a sixty-two-year-old Vietnamese grandfather, who was angry with his daughter, Kim, because she doesn't follow the "old ways" of his Buddhist religion. He is concerned that his grandchildren's lack of religion has severed their connection to their ancestors—him included. "My daughter married an American. They are raising my grandchildren as Unitarians, which I don't understand. All I know is that this religion doesn't respect ancestors or honor them as I do. This is sad, because respect for one's ancestors is woven into my religion. You see, my ancestors are very much alive for me. I talk with them every day. Now I will no longer be a part of my grandchildren's lives after I am gone. Will they ever talk with me after I am gone? Then what will happen to me?"

Kim, a hard working physician, is impatient with her father. "I am a modern woman, an American. I don't live in the past with all this hocus-pocus like my father. His old life has no relevance for me. I do not see any ancestors around in the hospital morgue. He is a wonderful, kind, and loving person. I am crazy about him. But his ancestor worship thing has no relevance to me or my children, although they don't seem to mind as much as I do. I am too busy to talk to my ancestors now; I am working ten hours a day and running a family."

There is no limit to the diversity of people, religions, races, and cultures that can be at odds over their beliefs. One journalist I know converted to Islam to marry Hind, a Muslim journalist he met in

Egypt. His family went "wild" about him marrying a "foreigner," until they grew to know and love Hind. Such "mixed" marriages may be hard to accept on both sides of the family at first, but love, kindness, and cute children always win out.

Learning Respect, Acceptance, and Compromise

We need to hone our skills in dealing with diversity. Tolerance, understanding, and acceptance will help us deal with any situation. When diversity becomes an issue with grandparents, we must try our best to honor and respect their beliefs and their strong need to pass them on to our child. For some grandparents, this is extra important. The trick is to be able to honor the grandparents' need and let our child know the reasons why we are doing this (thereby setting a great example, by the way).

If you personally encounter a similar situation, take the time to understand what grandparents think and feel. Then, in a loving and noncritical way, let them know how *you* feel as well. Share your beliefs and (if you feel negatively about theirs) why you think it would not be beneficial to your child to be inculcated with their religious and cultural legacy. If you can make the stretch, frame your child's exposure to their religious beliefs as being educational. This will give them license to teach your child their beliefs, without converting the child. If they can agree to such an arrangement, you have arrived at a win-win solution.

Parents need to know that children are not hurt by being exposed to a variety of belief systems. Actually, it broadens their perspective for children to be acquainted with diverse viewpoints and to learn to respect other people's views. We have to show them the way.

In Noreen's case, mentioned previously, she felt sorry for her mother, but at the same time she was committed to having her child adhere to her own agnosticism until the child could choose for herself. "I love my mother, but I can't give in to something I don't believe in," she said, "and I am not going to feel guilty about it." Allowing her child to learn about her mother's religion, but not adhering to it, is a good win-win option as long as her mother "signs" a nonproselytizing agreement.

In Mordecai's case, his daughter-in-law, Chantal, is a kind and generous person. She is quite open-minded and respectful of Sam's religious and cultural heritage. She resolved their differences by accommodating Mordecai's desire to teach his grandchildren about his religious beliefs. She went the extra mile by learning about Judaism herself.

"I do not object to grandpa teaching my daughter about Judaism. She is well aware of the fact that her father is Jewish, although Sam is not a practicing Jew. I am trying to show her similarities in our beliefs. For example, Christ was a Jew. We try to share holidays. My family spends Christmas at my parents' house and Passover at Mordecai's house. When my daughter is old enough, she can make her own religious choices."

What was Mordecai's response? "Half a loaf is better than none. My granddaughter will know a little about who I am, and what Judaism means to me. That is better than nothing. And I get to show her off in the synagogue once in a while on Saturday morning."

Likewise Kim and her father were able to reach a positive arrangement. Kim called a family meeting and made her feelings strongly known to Thanh. Her husband pitched in, urging Kim to "keep the old guy happy."

As a result, Kim let up and allowed her father to teach the children about his religious rituals (which they loved). "If I even get through to one child," Thanh said, "I'll have someone to talk to after I'm gone." Kim said, "It's between father and the children. If they are happy, OK. I'm out of it."

Regional and Socioeconomic Diversity

Sonya, thirty-eight, was born and raised in Philadelphia. Her husband, Hal, forty, is from Mississippi. She and her in-laws have a clash of backgrounds—a regionally based cultural difference. "My in-laws are so different from me. They live in no more than a shack.

There are all kinds of animals around where they live. I am a city girl, and I am afraid for my children when we go to visit. The dirt, the forest, the snakes. So I don't want to visit."

Sonya is going to have to become a bit more flexible to keep her family team intact, and she knows it. "Well, my husband says that he will take our children alone to visit his parents, so I won't have to be unhappy, and he won't have to hear me complain. However, I don't think that would be good for our marriage, so I'll have to tough it out. But I'll sleep at a motel."

Nick, twenty-eight, while in therapy for an anxiety problem, brought up the fact that he was concerned about a significant difference concerning his in-laws. He said, "My in-laws are snooty, very rich, country club types. I am not used to their kind of people. I feel they look down on me, that I am not one of them. I feel uncomfortable with their friends—all big shots. And they want me to bring my kids up like them, and I don't like it, nor can I afford it." Nick, a self-made, moderately successful businessperson feels a socioeconomic-educational-cultural difference from his in-laws.

Gwen, his wife, twenty-eight, feels that "it's all in Nick's head. My parents are great. Sure they are Ivy League types but they are good people. Nick has got to get over this."

Nick is trying. "I guess I married over my head. It is not their fault after all. It is the similarities between us that matter. They really have not done anything. I am driving Gwen nuts. I will get over this, or I am going to blow my marriage over nothing. Maybe I should stop being so stubborn and try to learn something from them."

Racial Diversity

Racial diversity can be difficult for some grandparents to deal with (and especially those who were raised in more racist times). Such a situation requires parents to go slowly and wait for grandparents to come around.

Pat, forty-three, a black classical singer, and Jim, forty-five, a Japanese violinist, have been married for fifteen years. Looking back,

Jim said, "Both families threw us out when we got married. I was temporarily disowned. But Pat's parents softened after a while. Then when our first child came along, things got better with my parents. Now with three children, and both Pat and I only children, things are almost back to normal. We just never gave up. However, it takes time. Lots and lots of time. Pat and I were the first ones ever in our families to break the color and race line. Fortunately, love conquers all, and having adorable kids helps. My family is of many colors."

Love melts all differences. So whether parents have an interracial alliance, or an adopted child is of another race, the most important thing parents can do to erase differences is to nurture the vital connection between the grandparent and child. This allows time for God, nature, love, or whatever else you may believe in (or not) to take over. I have rarely found it otherwise.

For example, Ariana, thirty-five, met and married Lyle, thirty-seven, in Italy when he was studying cooking there. They are both executive chefs; she is white and he is black. They have two, in his words, "very light-skinned" children, Brianna, four, and Nicholas, six. Lyle comes from a very religious, and "racist," Southern Baptist family in Mississippi.

Lyle knew he was going to have a problem getting his family to understand why he had married a white girl. When he first brought Ariana home, his family was upset. "My parents are still living in the fifties," Lyle said. "They remember the civil rights scene and are still angry at white people and holding on to the bitterness like bulldogs. When I brought Ariana home to meet them, they didn't know what to make of her. Her Italian accent and lack of any racist agenda or self-consciousness made her different from any whites they ever knew. So they were polite, but standoffish. After the kids were born, we visited several times a year. One of the things we love to do is to go to church together and be involved in church activities as a family. Now we are all pretty dark skinned, and my kids have olive skin. They can pass for white. My parents were embarrassed at first for all of us to go to church together. Well, Ariana said she wanted to go to church as a family. After my brothers and their wives agreed, mom and dad gave in. It was something for my parents to hold my kids' hands in church with everyone staring at them. You should have seen Ariana and my mom singing together. The kids had a ball. There were no more problems after that day. My mom told me she learned something that day and that God helped her accept it all. She said nice people are all that count."

Diversity Guidelines

Jim and Lyle echo the sentiments of Pavlov, the great Russian scientist, who recommended the course of *gradualness* in all things. Diversity is becoming a way of life that all of us have to deal with. Here are some guidelines for managing such situations effectively:

- Think carefully through our own beliefs and values and our ethnic and religious identity and choices.
- Assess our own prejudgments, intolerant attitudes, and prejudices. Isolate and recognize any "programmed" biases or prejudices.
- Assess the same for the grandparents. In addition, try to put yourself in the grandparents' shoes.
- Determine which of our beliefs and values fit with those of the grandparents and which are different.
- Make a commitment to address the differences and formulate a family policy for dealing with them.
- Call a family conference to discuss the issue. Explain our views concerning the diversity issue (religion, ethnicity, and so forth) and what they mean to us. Explain that we are open to learning about other aspects and ways of dealing with what we believe. Ask the same of the grandparents.
- Assert that the best way to resolve conflicts generated by diversity is to become a student of the other side. (This is a great message for children.)
- Set the example for the family concerning acceptance, tolerance, understanding, and respect.

Mutual respect, understanding, and attitudinal change are the keys to turning this highly charged issue into a wonderful learning opportunity for everyone. Exposure to different ways of thinking, believing, and worshipping can be very educational. Our child learns to be understanding and tolerant and learns how to embrace diversity by witnessing how we lovingly and respectfully work through this issue with grandparents. And isn't this what religion and family values are all about in the first place?

Gay and Lesbian Issues

Sometimes a member of the family team is homosexually oriented. In the past, homosexuals were hesitant to become parents. In fact, many homosexual persons stayed "in the closet" and never announced their sexual orientation to their loved ones. Not so today. According to (approximate) census figures, there are well over one million homosexual couples in the United States today. It is further estimated that between six to ten million children are being raised by at least one homosexual parent.

The whole idea of homosexual parenthood alone can make for conflicts with grandparents. Another twist concerns having a gay or lesbian grandparent as a member of the family team. If what follows does not apply to you specifically, I urge you to read on anyway. I assure you that what follows not only will be informative but also will enlighten you about some fascinating changes that are happening in our society today.

Homosexual Parents Dealing with Grandparents

An unprecedented number of homosexual men and women are becoming parents through adoption or reproductive technology. As a result, they are making their often-surprised (although happy) parents into grandparents. This remarkable event not only has brought "newly minted" homosexual parents into mainstream parenthood but also has helped many of them reconcile past differences with their parents and other family members.

For example, Glen knew he was gay when he first experienced "strange feelings" in the boys' locker room at junior high school. Although he dated girls, he knew that he was "different." He had his first homosexual encounter in college. His very traditional and loving parents' suspicions about his homosexuality grew stronger as the years passed, but nothing was said. When he "came out" and announced to his family that he was gay, they became upset and confused and withdrew from him. He felt hurt, abandoned, and misunderstood. "I didn't want to be gay," he said. "But I was."

After college, Glen moved to Los Angeles. After several years of minimal personal contact with his family, except for his grandmother (and considerable professional success as a film editor), Glen returned home to visit his grandmother when she became seriously ill. During the visit, he and his mother tearfully reconciled. His father, however, held back. He was continuing to struggle with the pain and disappointment he felt about his son's sexual orientation and the love he felt for Glen: not an easy task for men of his generation.

As time went on, Glen found a soul mate in Joel. After seven years together, Glen expressed to Joel that he had always wanted to have a family and was ready to have a child. After talking over their options, they decided to adopt a child. When Glen's parents heard about his intention to adopt, his mother told me that she "freaked out." She said, "How can he raise a baby with no mother?"

After the baby, Mikey, arrived, Glen became active in the local church that had consecrated his relationship with Joel. He wanted to have Mikey baptized. Now the head of a two-generational family, Glen wanted to add the third, grandparent, component. So he invited his parents to the baptism, hoping to have them bond with his son. It worked. Here is what Glen's father said about his "epiphany" while attending his grandson's baptism:

"I looked at my son and saw his pride at being a father. All of my negative attitudes and prejudices melted away. It is hard to express. When I saw Glen and Mikey, I knew how I had to be and what I had to do. Glen had made me a grandfather. I worried about Glen all of my life, about what was going to become of him. I had to get over my own limitations, how I felt about homosexuals. God knows, I have come a long way. Now I knew everything was going to turn out OK—a bit different from what I had envisaged—but OK all the same."

Glen's mother was concerned about the idea of the baby's not having a mother. Glen said, "He's got you." Glen's parents' experience is similar to that of other grandparents whose love for their child helped them become more open to diversity.

Parenthood offers an opportunity for homosexual persons (especially those separated or alienated from their families of origin) to enter the family mainstream, rally its members, and become a three-dimensional parent. The child is the key. Parenthood is a new beginning. It signals a beginning for reconciliation, or at least an attempt at resolving old family conflicts. The newly minted grandparents are challenged to reexamine intolerant attitudes and prejudices and expand their sense of tolerance, compassion, and understanding toward the new parent's life and parenthood.

The new parents may also have to help other family members deal with the same kinds of feelings. For homosexual parents, their own parents hold the key to the door of the family home. Reticent or confused siblings of a homosexual person will often look to their parents as an example of how to act in such a situation. When great-grandparents and grandparents set a positive example, younger people follow.

If you are a homosexual parent, your goal is to get the new grandparents to support your role as a parent, become educated concerning homosexual issues, and perhaps even become advocates for your child. Joining support groups can help too. For example, Parents, Families, and Friends of Lesbians and Gays (PFLAG) and other organizations that I've included in the Resources section are an important source for support and networking. Many grandparents are involved as well.

Benefits of Three-Dimensional Parenting to Children of Gay Parents

Three-generational parenting supersedes all other subcategories of parenting. Therefore when you get grandparents on your family team, you can assuage their concerns about any negative effect of homosexual parenting. Research is sparse in this area, but the research that does exist points to the importance of having grandparents offer opposite gender roles for children of homosexual parents.[2] My clinical experience has taught me that a loved child is a well child, no matter who does the loving.

Most of the children that I have met who were being raised by homosexual parents were untroubled if they had loving parents and an expanded family team. The family team fills all of the children's natural needs, as Rashida, twenty-two, points out: "When I was twelve years old, I played soccer," said Rashida, who was raised by "two mothers." "Most of the time, Mama Lee took me to practice. But when she had to travel for business, Mama Janet took me. My girlfriends were trying to figure out why I called them both mama and asked me where my father was. I said I did not have a father, but I had a large family with uncles and a grandfather. Therefore when the kids started to look at me funny, I just asked my grandfather to come to practice with me. Both of my mamas thought that was great. I do not mind being raised by two mothers; actually, it's pretty cool. But I need my uncles and grandfather too."

Guidelines and Suggestions for Homosexual Parents

If you are a homosexual parent or are considering becoming one in the near future, it is important that you begin to think three-dimensionally. Here are some ideas and suggestions to help you on whatever path you choose to parenthood:

- Get grandparents involved as early as possible in the prenatal process.
- Listen to their feelings about what you intend to do. Refer them to support groups or sources of information (see Resources).
- Discuss with them in depth how you are going about becoming a parent—adoption, technology, and so forth—so they become informed grandparents.

- Make sure grandparents are there when your child arrives so you become a three-dimensional parent from the beginning.

- Get them involved in your child's world and in the support system for homosexual families (PFLAG, for example).

- Bring your child into the life of all your family members.

Straight Parents Dealing with a Gay or Lesbian Grandparent

Homosexual grandparents have two origins. The first is seamless and smooth—when a homosexual parent's child has a child. In this situation, grandparenthood unfolds in a traditional manner, and for the most part, it is devoid of the sexual issues and complexities that can complicate homosexual parenting. The second way is when a formerly "traditional" parent comes out late in life, announcing his or her gay or lesbian status. This can be very painful and confusing for the family, and especially for the children and grandchildren.

It is not uncommon today to meet older people who have suppressed their homosexual feelings and longings throughout the early decades of their lives. During their later years, some have done a major turnabout and have gathered up the courage to announce their homosexual orientation to their families and the world.

Many of these people were involved in traditional marriages, became parents, raised their children, and lived a typical life in their families and communities. Whether or not they are married, widowed, or divorced at the time they announce their homosexuality, the news usually causes a great deal of turmoil and consternation in the family, and often the community as well. Their family members react in a mixed way. Some are accepting, others rejecting, most bewildered. The way they react to the news depends on their belief system, the makeup of the family, the number of children and grandchildren involved, and innumerable other personal and social factors.

When the children of these late announcers grow up, marry, and have children, they make their own parents into grandparents—homosexual grandparents, to be precise. That is where the confusion and often the trouble can start. I want to emphasize that what happens from this point on is highly individualized. What results depends on the personalities of the individuals involved and how the family accepts grandma's or grandpa's coming out in the first place. The task for parents in such situations is to find a way to overcome whatever they feel and find the rightful place for the grandparent in the family team.

Here's an example: Malcolm, seventy-two, a widower, announced to his family after church on a Sunday morning that he was gay. After his two children and their families recovered from the shock, his children shunned him. His daughter, Edna, was "shocked beyond belief. I knew my dad was not athletic, sort of an intellectual, but I never thought he was gay. At first, I did not know what to tell my son, and he is crazy about his grandfather. My brother wants to kill my father, not literally, of course."

Malcolm said that he had homosexual feelings while he was married, but he was too "mired in my life at the time" to come out of the closet. "I waited until my wife died to come out publicly. I probably never would have come out if she lived. I loved her too much to hurt her like that. Now I know I have hurt my children. However, with the way attitudes are changing today, I hope and pray they will come around."

The last time I saw Edna, she seemed to be softening. "There are worse things in the world, I guess. He is still my father. My son wants to see him. He says being gay is no big deal nowadays. Maybe he is more advanced than I am. I will try. But it's hard. I have so many bad thoughts about what homosexuals do." The last time I saw her, Edna was moving forward and working on accepting her father as he is. Malcolm is still keeping in touch with all of his family in spite of the infrequent feedback he receives.

Some parents that I know have been more successful than Edna in maintaining their family team under such circumstances. Ned, a sixty-two-year-old detective and a grandfather with ten grandchildren, "fell in love" with a younger man, a public defender, when Ned was forty. Five years later, he divorced his wife and moved in with his new partner. His five sons were very angry at him at first. Since then, some have relented and currently are on speaking terms with him. The oldest two sons have six children between them. Ned has been an involved grandfather with his oldest son's children, although his partner is barred from seeing them. He has less contact with his second son's children because his daughter-in-law disapproves of his homosexuality. Ned is naturally unhappy about the situation but has decided to "watch and wait" to see how things develop.

His partner, Bill, said he "would like to be involved with Ned's family, but I am persona non grata."

Ned is respectful of his children's feelings. "I understand how everyone feels. But I couldn't live a lie anymore. This is the price I have to pay."

Ned's oldest son, Simon, a firefighter, says that he called his dad a fag when he was angry with him, but now "my attitudes are mellowing. He has always been a great dad, and he is a wonderful grandfather. It's not good for the kids to see me calling my dad bad names. All of us feel that the rug has been pulled out from under us, especially my mother. She still loves him. As a parent, I have to keep it all together. Live and let live. I try but it's not easy."

When acknowledged homosexual parents become grandparents, the transition is usually smooth because children already know the score. John, twenty-eight, was adopted and raised by two men. "My two dads were overjoyed when my wife and I told them that we were going to have a child. Actually, they went nuts. Robert, he is the motherly one, went on a shopping binge. My other dad stayed cool. Robert calls my wife every day to see how she is doing. He wants to be with her when the baby comes. Her mother wants to be there too. That is going to be a scene, but I am sure it will work out. We kid Robert and tell him that he is going to be a wonderful grandmother."

Guidelines for Having a Homosexual Grandparent

If you are searching for ways to include a homosexual parent on your family team, the following guidelines, gleaned from the experiences of others, may be of help:

- Assess the family's reaction to the news that a grandparent is gay or lesbian. If everything is "copasetic," let well enough alone.

- Assess the children's experience and impressions. Discuss the matter openly and freely.

- Emphasize that sexuality has little to do with grandparenting.

- Try to keep the grandparent-grandchild bond as unaffected as possible. The younger the child, the easier it will be. In fact, younger children do not need to know anything concrete until they are able to understand the situation.

- Have the partner, when there is one, wait in the family wings and gradually come into the family's life as the comfort level rises. (See the discussion in Chapter Eight on stepgrandparenting for guidelines on handling this adjustment with sensitivity and patience.)

After we create our family team and do what is necessary to keep it running smoothly, we are ready to reap its benefits. Not only do we enjoy the positive benefits of having grandparents to make our life better, but we also have them available to us in times of need. With a family team, we can always call 1-800-grandparents for help to access grandparent solutions for our needs and problems. I will discuss how, why, and what we can use them for in the next chapters.

PART THREE

Grandparent Solutions

10

Asking for Practical Help

We all need help from time to time. Sometimes we just need a friendly ear, a pat on the back, or a cheerleader to encourage us. Other times, we need more intensive emotional, logistical, or even financial assistance. And if it all gets to be too much, we might even need someone to spell us for a while in caring for our child. We might even need someone to care for us.

Accessing help is no problem for three-dimensional parents. All we have to do when we need help is to turn to the grandparents on our family team for assistance. A grandparent's love, caring, and support offer both short- and longer-term solutions for what ails us. Over the years, I have seen grandparents in close families respond to the needs of their children and grandchildren in varied and wonderful ways.

To Ask or Not to Ask

Although it would seem completely natural—when we consider how nature has structured the family—that the first people we would instinctively ask for help are our own parents, many of us are hesitant to do so: some for good reasons, some not.

Bryna and Bob, both thirty-six, have a good reason to ask for help. They have three children, and both work full-time. Bob works at night; Bryna works during the day. They are overworked and tired, or more accurately, as Bob says, "exhausted."

Although Bob's parents live in the same city, he won't ask them to help on more than an emergency basis. Why? Because Bob has a lot of pride. He thinks in a typically two-dimensional way—that he needs to do everything by himself. For Bob, asking for help is an admission of weakness. Furthermore (and to his credit), by not asking for help, he feels he is being considerate of his parents' well-being. These incongruent views and attitudes—pride and consideration—block him from asking for help.

"We will handle things ourselves," he says. "My parents were hardworking farmers: seven days a week, eighteen hours a day, all of their lives. They deserve a rest."

When I asked Bob's parents how they felt about the hectic pace of Bryna and Bob's life, they expressed nothing but sympathy. His mother said, "We worked hard, sure, but we did it in the same place. They are all over the place. How they have a love life beats me. We want to help, but Bob is pigheaded like my husband. It runs in his family. He wants to do things his way. To him, asking for help means he is not up to the task. Ridiculous. We would be glad to pitch in more than we do, but we can't force ourselves on them."

I met Belle, thirty-seven, with four children, when she asked me to treat one of her children who was distraught after Belle's husband was killed in an automobile accident. Belle's parents had moved away to retire several years before the tragedy. When I suggested to Belle that she ask her parents to come back home to help, she nixed the possibility out of hand. Like Bob, who respects his parents and doesn't want to bother them, Belle had put her parents "out to pasture." "My parents worked hard all of their lives and deserve to take it easy."

Her parents (and in-laws as well, who were also retired and geographically unavailable) were quite concerned about how she was managing. Belle had given me permission to speak directly with them if they called to inquire about their grandson's condition. When her parents finally called, I was happy to tell them that their grandson was on the mend. During the conversation, I answered their concerns about Belle and her children. I said that although Belle was managing passably, she could use their hands-on support with the children.

"We would be happy to come back and help; we are sending money but I don't see how that is enough," her father said. I mentioned that he might make his offer directly to Belle. Her father called back two days later. "It took a bit of convincing but we are coming back."

After their return, life got a lot better for Belle and their grandchildren. Belle thanked me for being a go-between for her. "I didn't have the guts to ask them myself," she said.

Experience tells me that healthy and well-adjusted grandparents are happy to respond positively to parents' request for assistance. If we don't ask, we will never know. Of course, asking for help isn't easy. It requires a major effort to overcome feelings of pride and can be especially hard when old child-parent issues get in the way. Nevertheless grandparents offer us the best help possible. That's why we have to try to get rid of the "I-will-do-it-all-by-myself" nuclear family mentality, or the idea that asking for help means personal failure, or the notion that obtaining grandparents' assistance, interest, and involvement opens the door to intrusiveness and meddling. In the three-dimensional family team, our "one-for-all-and-all-for-one" credo makes it normal and natural for everyone to help everyone else upon request and give it all they've got. No guilt trips allowed. Cast thy bread upon the waters and all that jazz.

In this chapter and the one following, we'll discuss a variety of situations where it is appropriate to ask grandparents for practical, financial, and emotional help (although it is sometimes difficult to separate these categories from one another). I cannot emphasize strongly enough that when we include grandparents in a supportive role, it not only fulfills their function on our family team but also supplies a wonderful example for our children.

By freely asking our parents for help, we give our own children permission to ask us for help should they need it in the future. And remember, what goes around comes around.

When a Child Is Born

For many years, I have been advocating that parents invite grand-parents to the birth of a new child. I base this suggestion on my experience that all of the parents I have met over the past three decades who have allowed their own parent or in-law to attend the birth of their child—whether they were in the delivery room, right outside the delivery room, pacing the waiting room floor, rushing to get to the hospital, or even on the telephone during the process—found it a joyful, unforgettable, and even magical experience. And so did the grandparents!

Inviting grandparents into the delivery room is the best. One grandmother, Ila, fifty-three years old, put it well: "What a bonding experience I had with my own daughter. I was in the delivery room with her. Her husband was helping her with her breathing and pushing. Her dad was waiting outside the delivery room door because my daughter is modest. When the baby was born, I was speechless. The doctor tossed him up on my daughter's chest, and I touched him. My grandson! I looked deep in my daughter's eyes, and I tell you I never had such a feeling before—I am tearing when I think of it. Then I backed off and let her have her moment together with my son-in-law."

Her daughter agreed. "I know what mom means. It was different from the joy I felt with my husband. There was something in mom's eyes at that moment. I felt it down to my toes. Y'know, I came out of her and my baby comes out of me. What a wonder! I never realized before it happened what a wonderful experience it is to have her by my side. It's just something I never thought about before."

If you can make an effort to go beyond any reluctance to having a family member witness your child's birth, try it out. Of course, respect your comfort and modesty level. In any case, include grand-parents in the process in the way that you find most comfortable. Grandma and grandpa do not have to be looking over the doctor's shoulder at the moment of birth. They can be waiting outside the door, right there to hold their grandchild in those first few precious minutes of life. Making them participants in the event is what counts.

Many of us have family members spread all over the country, so what do we do if grandparents cannot physically attend the birth? The good news is that we can do more today to include them, thanks to technology, than ever before in human history. With a video camera and tape recorder or digital photography and the Internet, we can show them the moment the baby comes into the world, the parents' joy, and the first family photo within minutes of the birth.

Plan for grandparents to visit and help you before, or as soon as possible after, the baby comes. Cherry, thirty-four, let her parents know the date when her Caesarean section was scheduled so they could be there early and remain to help. "I live in North Carolina. My parents live in Phoenix. My mom and dad are coming out a week before my Caesarean to look after my son and daughter. This way, I can familiarize them with my apartment and the way I do things. I am making lists, lots of lists." If you are expecting an adopted child, getting grandparents involved from the beginning is very important as well.

Here are some general guidelines for including the grandparents in the birth of your child:

- Include grandparents from the beginning of the pregnancy.
- Invite them to participate and help during the pre- and post-natal periods. Have them tag along when you go to the doctor or get an ultrasound. Educate them about modern obstetrics and child care.
- Allow them to assist in planning and purchasing what you will need for your child.
- Have them attend the birth of your child according to your comfort level. Can grandmother watch the delivery? Can grandfather be in the delivery room and see the baby after it comes out and is placed in a position that will not threaten

the modesty of the mother? Should grandfather wait outside? It may be helpful to consult the obstetrical team for advice.

- Use technology to involve long-distance grandparents in the process. Use *videoconferencing* (a video camera that plugs into the computer) or digital pictures to get the baby's first pictures over the wires quickly. Record baby's first sounds and play them over the phone.

- If grandparents live far away and plan to attend the birth, plan the time and place of their stay with them.

- Make the birth of the baby a family affair. Coordinate your wishes and actions with all grandparents and family members.

- Use the same plan for welcoming a new adopted grandchild.

- If you have other children, ask them to baby-sit for you when you go for doctor appointments or need to rest.

- Arrange for grandparents to take care of the children while you are in the hospital, and for the first two weeks postpartum.

Becoming a parent is a family affair—a momentous and life-changing event. This applies to us, our partner, and all of our parents. A new baby offers a chance to form a new family team, to forgive the past and start anew. By getting grandparents involved from the beginning, in a practical and helpful way, we assure our new family of strong underpinnings that will help us meet any future challenges.

This support is especially important for new mothers, who can count on the new grandmothers as experts in the field. Even though new child-care theories emerge with every generation, the old ways still hold true. For example, when Ida, twenty-one, took her new baby home from the hospital, she became alarmed when her infant did not open her eyes while she was feeding. Panicky, Ida called the hospital emergency room. She tearfully told the nurse what was going on. "My baby doesn't open her eyes," Ida sobbed. The nurse thought for a moment and said, "Did you call your mother?"

Baby-Sitting

Every parent needs a break. That's where grandparents come in. One of the greatest sources of help that grandparents can give us is a bit of respite from child care once in a while. This is a natural and enjoyable job for most grandparents. It's what they do. Indeed for most of human history, grandparents have cared for the young while parents were out in the world trying to hunt, plant the crops, or keep the fires burning. Today we call this baby-sitting. Most of us would prefer that our parents care for our child when we need it, as opposed to putting the child in a day-care center or hiring an expensive baby-sitter. The reasons are obvious: child and grandparents have fun, we have peace of mind, and it costs less.

Most of the time, baby-sitting is a win-win situation. At other times, baby-sitting can generate conflicts. Parents naturally want their own routine to be followed. Grandparents may have other ideas. So to make grandparent baby-sitting work most effectively, we need to reconcile our differences. We do this via good, open, and direct communication and mutual respect. With these qualities, we can resolve any conflicts or issues that come up. Here is one example of some issues that can come up with baby-sitting, as described by Nora, twenty-six:

> I have an ongoing problem between my daughter, who is two years and one month, and my mum. My mum and dad have been fantastic and started looking after my daughter from when she was about six months at their house. It was only one day a week, while I went to work. I worked from home the rest of the time. By the time she was nearly one, my job changed, and I had to work about three days in the office. So I had her in child care (big mistake) and at my mum and dad's two days a week.
>
> Child care was awful; my daughter hated me leaving her, and I was heartbroken every time I left. I decided that I would only work in the office two days a week, and she would then

be at my mum and dad's only. Since she was about twelve months or so, she has begun to show a dislike toward my mum, and I have no idea why. Recently, she has become aggressive toward her, pushes her out of the room, and tells her to go away. She does this even when my mum is just visiting or I am just visiting her. She does it in front of our family and friends and my mum is embarrassed by it, and I can understand why.

I can only think that she sees my mum as taking her away from me. She is not like that with my dad though. She adores him, and I know he does spend a lot of the day that she is there playing with her, whereas my mum would be busy doing the housework, etc., and attend to my daughter for feeding, changing, etc.—the practical things.

I will note though that when no one else is around, my daughter understands that "grandma will have to do." Another point I will make is that I know that my mum "favors" her other grandson (my nephew), and I can see it happening very subtly while my daughter is there too, and I'm wondering if this happening on occasion would be enough for her to dislike her in some way. My nephew is there the same time as my daughter probably one day out of every two or three weeks, so not often. I mentioned this to my mum, but she became defensive about having a favorite and said I was being silly and that my daughter was too young to realize that anyway.

Fortunately, after a good discussion with her "mum," Nora felt better. She was reassured that her mother has no favorites and would persevere in her efforts to help. Her mother felt better too. She felt that Nora "wasn't herself" but didn't know why. "I am so glad that Nora unburdened herself to me. After all, how am I to know if I am doing something wrong if she doesn't tell me. I am not perfect and I know it." When we don't communicate with the other person, our imagination takes over. And that is often for the worst.

Finding the Right Balance

Some considerate parents feel troubled about imposing on their own parents when they ask them to baby-sit. Such feelings can be worked out by asking directly if the grandparent feels imposed upon. Of course, some busy grandparents do feel imposed upon. Some grandparents that I have met complained of feeling "exploited" or "used" by their children. Some are so busy that they have little time to baby-sit. This can be most disappointing for a parent who needs a break. Often the solution lies in finding a proper balance.

Melsene, fifty-seven years old, is one single grandmother who feels "exploited." Her daughter and son-in-law want her to baby-sit their two children almost every weekend. Melsene complains that her daughter is asking too much. "I have a life of my own too. My daughter tells me that she and her husband need time together. But I feel like they are putting their parental responsibilities on my back. I love being with my grandchildren, but I work all week too and need time for myself."

Conversely, Melsene's daughter says, "I remember my grandmother helping my mother all the time—bringing food for breakfast every weekend, always at our house. I love my mother dearly, she is a wonderful person. It is just that I expected that she would be like my grandmother."

Melsene and her daughter are out of balance and help is needed. A little more consideration on Melsene's daughter's part would help. After a long talk, they agreed that Melsene would baby-sit one day on the weekend on a regular basis but would be available for emergencies. "It's not so bad," Melsene said. "When the kids get older, I can take them wherever I want to go."

Pedro, forty-two, solved a similar problem with his father. "When my wife died, I asked my father to come over every afternoon and look after my kids after they came home from school. He is retired and hangs out with his buddies most of the day. I asked him nicely, expressed that I need him to help for a while, and to his credit, he did. But he was grouchy about it. Not to the kids, but to me. What I had to do is take him out at night for a couple of drinks and tell him how much I appreciated his efforts. I also told him how much the kids love and respect him. After that, he changed. He told me he was proud of me for how hard I am working and especially about talking with him directly, and not complaining behind his back like so many people in his family do. Now we are closer."

Pedro found the best way to deal with his father. He used open and direct communication to establish a mutually acceptable—win-win—baby-sitting arrangement

How Children Feel About Grandparents' Baby-Sitting

Our children appreciate when we make the effort to have a grandparent that they love and care about baby-sit. Most grandchildren prefer grandparents to strangers, and especially if the grandparents are fun. Similar to the way they view parents, children view grandparents as permanent family fixtures: useful for love, caring, joy, safety, and support. In fact, with rare exceptions, most children that I know would choose the company of a grandparent over any other baby-sitter.

One humorous exception I came across was a twelve-year-old named Bert. Bert had a "killer" crush on the eighteen-year-old high school cheerleader who had been his baby-sitter since he was eight. "I have fun when my grandparents baby-sit, of course," he said, "but I like Patty to baby-sit me and my little sisters because she is so gorgeous and wears tight clothes." Enough said.

When grandparents baby-sit, it is a win-win-win situation. Here are some ideas and suggestions for getting any available grandparent to help:

- Sort out your own feelings about having a grandparent baby-sit. Do you have a good relationship? Are you trusting of the grandparent's health and capability to act in an emergency?
- Assess the practical availability of the grandparent. Does she work? Is he retired? Do they have the time and interest?

- Determine the logistics for baby-sitting. How much available time does the grandparent have?

- Have a meeting with grandparents to discuss your rules and regulations and what you expect from them. What kinds of food are to be consumed? What discipline is to be used? Does your child need tutoring or monitoring of homework?

- Whether you need grandparents to baby-sit once in a while or on a regular basis, make sure to have a backup plan (for another baby-sitter) if they cannot make it.

- Discuss and review the family baby-sitting plan on a regular basis. Make sure it works for everyone.

Asking grandparents to baby-sit is a gift for them. It allows them time alone with their grandchild to nurture their vital connection. Coordinating the process in a seamless way is good for the child too. The less hassle, the more the child is happy and secure. When conflicts arise, deal with them quickly, directly, and openly. Let the kids get a word in too, when appropriate.

Sending Your Child to Visit Grandparents

From time to time, and for many reasons, we may need to send a child to visit with a grandparent. This can be for fun, for health reasons, or because we need some respite. Many working mothers who travel frequently will often send a child to grandma's house for a period of time. This is different from baby-sitting, which usually takes place at the parents' house.

When we do send a child on a visit, it is normal to be concerned if grandma and grandpa are going to do things our way. "Is my child going to come back a hundred pounds overweight or completely spoiled?" we wonder. "Will my baby be safe?" "Has my mother forgotten how it is to have a small child in her home?" "Can my father keep up, with his diabetes?" "Will they give my child her vitamins?"

All of these worries, and more, can be put to rest if we prepare for our child's visit well in advance, foresee any potential difficulties, and develop a good plan. Giving grandparents clear instructions concerning what our child needs and expects, as well as supplying clear safety guidelines, makes things much easier. Here are some ideas and suggestions that I have found helpful for how to proceed:

1. *Plan ahead*. The key to a successful child visit is adequate planning and preparation. The first thing is to generate excitement and enthusiasm well in advance. Also plan what we are going to do while the child is gone. If we have more than one child, are they both going? Are we staying at home or will we be nearby? For example, some parents who send their child with the grandparents to our yearly Grandparent-Grandchild Summer Camp stay in nearby towns: on call, so to speak.

   When planning together with grandparents, make sure to share information about our child's medical, nutritional, or other needs. Make sure to fill out a medical-authorization form for the grandparents to use in case of any medical emergency where they would have to act in our stead.

   One grandfather learned how important this can be after his visiting grandson got a fishing hook stuck in his shoulder. When grandfather hastened his grandson to the hospital emergency room, the medical personnel refused to treat the child until they could talk with a parent on the phone. Fortunately, grandfather had his daughter's cell phone number handy and called her immediately. If your child is going to stay with grandparents for a protracted period, I recommend that you ask grandparents to take a course in CPR. It is especially helpful for dealing with accidents, choking, and administering first aid.

2. *Create a private place*. Depending on the grandparents' living conditions, ask them to make a special private, safe place for your child in their home—a place where the child can have

some privacy, rest, sleep, and have room to play. One grand-parent that I know, who lives in a modest apartment, has a special drawer for each grandchild in a "special" dresser that she has reserved for the grandchildren's use. From time to time, she puts something special in the drawer as a surprise. Each grandchild also leaves clothes and toys until the next visit. If a younger child is going to stay at grandma's for a while, it's a good idea to bring over the child's paraphernalia (crib, high chair, playpen, stroller, potty seat), or if grandma lives far away, have her rent what the child will need.

3. *Focus on safety.* We always worry about our child's safety, of course. The younger the child, the more we worry. So grand-parents will have to keep a close eye on the child. If the child is a toddler, have the grandparents get down on their knees and look at the rooms in their home from the eye level of the child. Remind them to stash the Wedgwood china and tie down the houseplants and other breakables and cherished objects, far from the reach of small hands. A grandchild will never get in trouble if there is nothing around to destroy.

A grandmother who collected colored glass ornaments found this out the hard way. Her toddling granddaughter, while delightedly exploring the (unchildproofed) living room, toppled over several of the ornaments, shattering one to smithereens. Of course, this made the child's parents unhappy and defensive too. Fortunately, grandma took the blame for not keeping things out of the child's way, learned from her mistake, got down on her knees, scoped out the room, and made the necessary changes. She even put a gate across the entrance to the living room. "That should do it for the next three years," she said.

Although grandparents already know a lot about safety, (because *we* are alive and kicking), it does not hurt to remind them gently that toddlers are susceptible to burns, falls, drown-ing, suffocation, poisoning, strangulation, and electrical shock.

So if they are going to have your toddler for a while, make sure they install gates at the top and bottom of stairways; remove items that could break and cause cuts from low-lying areas; lock cabinet doors that contain household cleaners, poisons, or medicines; put foam protectors on sharp edges of low tables; and whatever else you see. They should be especially careful about securing loose wires and blind and shade cords, and they should make sure to seal all electrical outlets in their home. When they run the bath for the child, they need to make sure to turn on the cold water first. Seat belts in the car are, of course, a must, as well as child safety seats: an ounce of prevention, and so forth and so on.

4. *Plan activities*. If grandparents are concerned about what they are going to do with the child, suggest they read together and supply some books. Suggest to grandparents that they create a small library for the child in their home and place her books next to their books. You may want to send along some school material too. Suggest that grandparents take a walk down memory lane with the child and pore over any family photo albums or old videos together. Children love to look at old pictures and hear the stories. Listening to music together is another great activity.

Playing board and card games is also a lot of fun. So make sure that grandparents have plenty of age-appropriate games on hand as well as drawing and painting supplies for younger children. We need to make sure that our child knows to pitch in and help the grandparents too (age appropriately, of course).

Summing up, here are some systematic reminders of what to do when your child is going to be with grandparents:

- Plan ahead. Give grandparents medical authorization to act for you in case of an emergency. Ask them to learn CPR.
- Talk about the visit well in advance with your child to generate enthusiasm and excitement.

- Inform grandparents to childproof their home according to your child's age.

- Tell your child to help.

- Let them know where you will be at all times.

- Give them permission to teach your child new skills or activities. She will remember the visit for the rest of her life.

- When the visit is over, plan for the next time.

Financial Aid

More and more parents today are asking grandparents for financial assistance. Of course, what grandparents are able or willing to supply depends on the quality of the relationship, the personalities of the people involved, and the resources of the grandparents. Grandparents with sufficient financial resources can help with a one-time expense (helping to buy a first home) or an ongoing expense (helping with school and college tuition or child care or supplementing a single parent's income). Chances are, whatever your parents' available resources, you have noticed a change in their spending behavior since they became grandparents. If they are like most other grandparents, they are experiencing an uncontrollable urge to "buy stuff" for your child. This urge is acknowledged by a great many grandparents that I have met, irrespective of how thrifty they are or how much, or how little, money they have.

I have joyfully named this strange "affliction" the "grandparent buying bug." This is a new and emerging syndrome, still ignored by members of the medical or psychological professions. That's why we don't see afflicted grandparents being quarantined. As a parent, you can capitalize on this affliction to benefit you and your child.

The buying bug is activated by the birth of a grandchild and tends to infect grandmothers first. This behavior occurs early because grandmothers understand what babies need and target their purchases to fulfill these needs. That's because they usually have more hands-on experience caring for babies. Although grandfathers usually will spring for a teddy bear, dollhouse, or computer when the baby is a bit older, many are confused by or uninformed about basic baby products. As a result, they can well end up buying clothes and toys that are the wrong size or not age appropriate for their grandchild. As the child gets older, grandfathers have more opportunities at hitting the jackpot with the right gift.

Afflicted grandparents can get into trouble with parents about the timing and the type of purchases they make. When high-priced items are involved, teamwork is necessary. Children should always understand that the big gifts come from both parents and grandparents. We don't want them to think that grandparents are an unlimited source of goodies, even though that may be true.

On a more serious note, it is a good idea to begin early in the child's life and collaborate with all of the grandparents (using available resources, of course) to create a family fund to be used for your child. Such funds can be used in many ways: to coordinate family gift giving and help parents purchase what the child really needs.

For example, before your new child arrives, determine what you need for the child and what you can personally afford to purchase. Then have a meeting with grandparents to let them know what you need and determine who will buy the things that you cannot personally supply: carriages, cribs, high chairs, furniture, car seats, and so forth.

By coordinating the grandparents' buying impulse, you can prevent overenthusiastic, but well-meaning, grandparents from purchasing things you do not need, do not want, or do not fit. Having your house filled with "stuff" that you don't want or need can be annoying.

When Fred, a sixty-seven-year-old grandfather, bought a large rocking horse for his grandson, there was really no place in his son's small apartment for it. The parents told Fred to take it back. He did not want to, saying, "I never had a rocking horse when I was a child, and I always wanted one like this one. I never could find one like this before, and I want my grandson to have one."

To avoid a fight, his daughter-in-law keeps the rocking horse in the basement of their building. She brings it out when Fred comes over. "Fred has his heart set on this rocking horse. I hate bringing it up and down from the basement, but it's worth not having a hassle with him."

Fred says, "I know they bring out the horse when I come over. But that's OK. At least my grandson can ride it when I am there."

Managing Grandparents' Spending

By preempting and managing a grandparent's natural urge to spend, you can make your life a lot easier. Martita, thirty-four, manages her parents' spending urge quite well, directing it toward the financial help she needs. "I had my first child when I was eighteen, and my parents had to help my husband and me. Every year, I tell them what we need, and we discuss how they can help. They help us with clothes and bicycles for the children and lots more. They are putting money aside for each child's college too."

Many grandparents today are paying for their grandchild's education and collaborating with parents to buy the big-ticket items. Dan, eighteen, said, "My grandparents and my parents both chipped in to buy me my jalopy for a high school graduation present. It's great! Except my grandmother is chicken to ride in it with me. But I'll get her yet."

Caroline, forty-three, a single mother with three children, asked her parents to pitch in to help her buy a house in a better neighborhood. "No problem," her father said. "I want my grandchildren to be in a safe neighborhood and to go to a good school. I don't like where they live now. Caroline is a single mother and needs our help. We don't have too much money, but what we have is to make our lives better. Caroline needs it now, not later on after the children grow up."

Don't be hesitant to ask grandparents who can afford it for help with time or money for medical, education, or quality-of-life costs. For example, when it was discovered that Samantha, six years old, had a reading problem, her grandparents paid for a learning specialist. Veronica, thirty-four, wanted to increase her quality of life by working one day a week and having grandparents baby-sit. Her parents lived more than 120 miles away and found it difficult to drive back and forth in one day. They couldn't sleep at Veronica's because her apartment had only two small bedrooms. Hotels were too expensive on a weekly basis. After putting their heads together, they decided that the grandparents would supplement Veronica's rent payment so she could move into a larger apartment where they could have their own room to stay overnight.

To be serious about the buying bug, it's really not all about money. You can ask grandparents to spend *time* as well as money. Emma, who lives in a trailer park, asked her mother, a seamstress, to make dresses for her girls. Her father, a carpenter, built an elaborate playhouse for the children (out of scrap lumber) in their small backyard. The possibilities for collaborating with grandparents for financial or any other kind of support are only limited by your ability to appropriately ask of them what is in their power to give.

Coordinating Grandparent Support

Now here is a tricky bit. If you are going to ask grandparents for help, and especially financial help, make sure to coordinate the contributions of both sets of grandparents as equitably as possible. It will take some planning and coordination to create such a grandparent "partnership." It helps for all of us to call a family meeting from time to time to state family members' needs and to figure out how grandparents can help. When one set of grandparents has more time and money than the other, it pays to spend a moment to figure out how to balance their gifts and contributions so that it remains a partnership. When it comes to longer-term and more complex financial matters—for example, wills, inheritances, trusts, and college funds—it is better to deal with each set of grandparents separately. It is important, however, to let the other set know what is going on, if not the financial details.

Although I have already addressed the issue of grandparent competition, it is important to keep the partnership idea in the forefront and to be as evenhanded as possible when finances are involved. Otherwise things can get contentious. One grandparent's babysitting may be as valuable as another's buying the family a new car.

Here are some further ideas and suggestions for taking advantage of grandparents' willingness—individually or as partners—to offer financial help:

- Make a habit of consulting with grandparents before using their services or purchasing gifts for your child, especially when it comes to items that are more expensive.

- Let grandparents know clearly what you personally want to purchase for your child: her first bicycle, his first baseball glove. This way, your special gift won't be usurped or upstaged by a more expensive model.

- Ask grandparents to purchase *legacy gifts* that your child can pass on to future generations—for example, a family portrait, a baby's first silver cup and spoon, a rocking horse, or a small rocking chair.

- Ask grandparents for time too. Grandparents who are handy can contribute their skills and labor. For example, some grandparents may be especially talented at assembling cribs or wallpapering a room, tasks that are greatly appreciated by working moms and dads.

- Balance each grandparent's contribution.

- Let the child know how grandparents are helping.

We can only ask for what grandparents can give. Therefore we cannot ask grandparents to help if they are not able. But what if grandparents *are* able to help and not willing to do so? What if a parent asks and is rejected?

Take Ryan, thirty-eight, for example, who asked his "wealthy" in-laws to help him put together enough money for a down payment on a home. His in-laws (who could well afford it) refused, saying that he should be able to live within his means. Similarly, Makayla, forty-one, a single working mother with a four-year-old child, asked her mother to help her pay for a cleaner for a half day once a week. Her mother refused, saying it was Makayla's responsibility to take care of her home. Then there's Leon, thirty-nine, father of two, who asked his own parents to help him with tuition for night accounting school and was refused because they were angry at him for dropping out of college and in his father's words, "throwing away my hard-earned money."

How do we know what grandparents are able to give? We can answer this question by asking them and—unless their inability to do so is quite clear—giving them the opportunity to say yes or no. I have seen more grandparents willing to help but who were not asked than the contrary—far more. So take a chance and ask. Remember also that a close grandparent-grandchild bond adds a dimension to the need that grandparents will perceive. Most grandparents want to help not only their children but their grandchildren as well.

If help is possible, don't give up after the first try. In the previous examples, Ryan and Makayla did not persevere in their requests and became angry toward the grandparents. Leon, in contrast, after recovering from the anger he felt about being rejected, tried again. He had to overcome his father's long-standing resentment about Leon's "wasting" his college tuition. So he took his father out to lunch and explained that he wanted to improve himself and raise his standard of living for his children (which went over well with his father). He asked forgiveness about wasting two years of college tuition. His father was touched and agreed to help. "I guess you have grown up," his father said. If his pride had gotten in the way, Leon would never have become an accountant.

If you ask grandparents for financial help, make it clear that there are no strings attached. Money is easily used as a method of intrusive control. When Jada, twenty-eight, asked her parents to lend her ten thousand dollars for a down payment on a home, she had to ward off her mother's overenthusiasm about choosing where and how she should live.

"My mother started calling real estate brokers in expensive neighborhoods, and we wanted a small tract house on a big street with lots of kids," Jada said. "I began to wonder what I was paying for this money. I had to sit down with mom and tell her that my husband and I were going to do this on our own and thanks a lot but stay out of it. That didn't go over too well. It took her a couple of months to get over it. Now all is back to normal."

It may be necessary to bury old resentments in order to ask. Actually, asking for help can sometimes undo wrongs of the past. Kelsey, thirty-seven, with three children, needed a bigger car. She told me, "It would be a cold day in hell before I will ask my parents for help." Kelsey was angry with her parents because she felt that she was the "Cinderella" of her family, that her parents preferred her sister and brother to her and were freer in offering them help. Consequently, as a teenager, Kelsey "couldn't wait to get out of the house and be on my own." She left home at eighteen and got a job in a small, local real estate firm. In spite of her anger, she remained in the same town as her parents and saw them often. Her parents felt that Kelsey was born with a chip on her shoulder. Three years after she left home, Kelsey met and married her husband, Chip.

Kelsey and her husband were making ends meet but had no extra income. Now they needed twenty-five hundred dollars for a down payment for a small family van. They could afford the monthly payments but couldn't scrape up a down payment and had nowhere else to turn. When Kelsey finally asked her parents to help, they were happy to do so, which, Kelsey said, "blew my mind."

Her parents were aware that they hadn't treated Kelsey as well as they would have liked. Her mother said, "I have always felt bad about Kelsey. She was what you call now an ADD kid, always on the move. She drove us crazy. I found myself constantly yelling at her and I didn't want to. Helping her now makes me feel better." Kelsey was pleased as well.

The bottom line is that asking for reasonable financial help under difficult circumstances can't hurt. Actually, you might be doing grandparents a favor. Offering help can give grandparents an opportunity to make up for past mistakes and renew family love and commitment. If we don't try, we may be missing an opportunity to strengthen our bonds. What is good for parents is good for children. It is good for children to see grandparents helping the family.

In the next chapter, I will present more about the most important areas in which you can ask grandparents for help. I will discuss grandparents who offer solutions for the emotional needs of parents who are going through difficult times.

11

Asking for Emotional Support

Some situations where parents need to ask their own parents for help include times fraught with emotional pressures that may tax parents severely—for example, when it comes to dealing with the frustration of being unable to have a biological child and having to adopt, or when raising a child with special needs, or when needing help during a difficult period with a child. Situations such as divorce and sickness, where it is often impossible to keep things afloat without assistance, are suited for asking for grandparents' assistance. And raising a child alone, especially in adverse conditions, can be exhausting, so we may need grandparents to spell us from child care for a period. Emotional support can be accessed over distance as well, so "long-distance" grandparents can be helpful too.

The Grandparents' Role in Adoption

As happy as the outcome may be, the initial decision, as well as the process of adoption itself, can be very stressful. The more support a prospective adoptive parent can get, the better.

The difficulties involved in making the adoption decision, finding a child, welcoming the child home, and introducing the child to the family are considerable. The stress is similar whether the reason for adopting is an inability to produce a biological child (which has its own complex stressors) or a personal choice to forgo having a biological child and adopting one instead. The "expectant" grandparents can help by offering love, understanding, and emotional support for parents as they go through the adoption process and beyond. If you have an adopted child, are considering adoption, or have a friend in an adoptive situation, the following discussion will assist you in using grandparents' help.

Grandparents can help early during the adoption decision process when parents often need a friendly ear to share their thoughts, feelings, and experiences. However unwarranted they may be, feelings of guilt, inadequacy, frustration, sadness, and anger often plague couples who are frustrated in their ability to conceive a child on their own.

As many of us know, the process of dealing with the failure of trying to conceive a child—with its interminable visits to the doctor, its "medicalization" of sexuality, and the anxiety and disappointment that accompany repeated attempts and failures to conceive—is highly stressful and emotionally and physically exhausting. Parents who are going through such an experience need love and support. That is why grandparents can serve as an enormous source of comfort. To be most helpful, they need to be involved early in the process. By so doing, parents lay the groundwork for the family team, even before the team is constituted.

Couples who have been frustrated in their attempt to conceive need to spend some time to process the psychological loss and disappointment involved. After they have mourned their loss, it is time to consider their next option. Do they resign themselves to remain childless, or do they consider adoption?

This is where a grandparent's role is critical: in nurturing, supporting, and comforting the couple as they go through the decision-making process. It took Martin, forty, and Maxine, thirty-six, over seven years to finally agree to adopt. "After five years of trying," Maxine said, "I was ready to commit suicide . . . between taking my temperature day and night, the unromantic planned sex, doctor's visits, in vitro attempts that never took, tons of money, and God knows what else. I tell you, I could not have made it without my mother. I asked her to help and to come with me whenever Martin could not make it to the doctor.

"My time with my mom, the lunches where I cried my heart out, saved me. She was always there, day or night, with plenty of tissues at the ready because I would cry at the drop of a hat. Mom went through everything with me hand in hand. My father helped too. When we decided to adopt, mom was happy. That made me feel better because I was having a sense of failure . . . you know . . . I could not give her a biological grandchild. I know I shouldn't feel like that but I did. And when we got our baby, she was as eager as we were. Now my family is complete."

Educating Grandparents About Adoption

If you intend to adopt a child, include grandparents in the planning and actual adoption process. You might start by calling a family meeting. Educate them about the different types of adoption and which type you are choosing. For example, explain to your parents the difference between a closed adoption (birth parents unknown to the adoptive family) and an open adoption (birth parents known).

"I told my father we were going to choose an open adoption," said Maureen. "He expressed his reservations. He had these visions of the biological parents coming to visit their child and him wanting to go home with them instead of staying with our family. I had to assure him that will not happen. After he relaxed, he became a great help to me. Now he is my son's best friend after his dad."

The increase in the adoptions of foreign children is something parents are talking over with grandparents as well. I referred to this in a previous chapter on diversity (see Chapter Nine).

Grandparents will want to know about the background of an adopted child. Is the child healthy, or does it have special needs? Take the initiative to educate them by giving them adoption books or guiding them to talk to other families who have adopted. Numerous sites on the Internet provide information about all aspects of adoption (see Resources).

The support you get from grandparents will be much more effective when you allow them to discuss their personal feelings about the adoption with you. Expect their reactions to differ according to the circumstances of the adoption. Some may have more trouble if a child is from another culture—although I really have not seen this to be a serious problem. Children eventually win everyone over.

When You Choose to Adopt

Grandparents might be hard put to understand if you *choose* to adopt even though you are able to have children of your own. When adopting is a choice for you, not a necessity, you will not experience any disappointment about not being able to conceive. However, your own parents might be concerned that their genes will not be passed on through the family bloodline.

If you are single or homosexual, you may suffer additional stress because of the possible lack of support (or downright disagreement) for this choice from your family. Even though societal attitudes toward parents who are single by choice and toward diverse families are changing for the better, there is still a way to go before single, or homosexual, parents achieve the same acceptance (in some quarters) that the so-called traditional family now claims. Either way, however, chances are, you will create an overjoyed grandparent.

One grandmother, Sylvie, fifty-eight, told me, "Because my daughter is gay, I always figured grandchildren were out of the question. But when my daughter and her partner decided to adopt a child, well, what can I say? My husband and I were stunned at first, then confused, then just overjoyed. And we sure love that baby."

Special Issues with the Expectant Adoption

Awaiting the arrival of a child is always an exciting and energizing process. There are some differences, however, between what happens when expecting a biological child and awaiting the arrival of an adopted one. These differences are important to consider in using grandparents' help.

The birth of a biological grandchild is preceded by the announcement of pregnancy. The announcement heralds a happy occasion: celebrations are in order! Other family members eagerly anticipate the arrival of the child and share in the day-to-day progress of the pregnancy. Celebrations and activities such as baby showers, fixing up a room for the baby, buying the necessities, can heighten the anticipation. Expectant parents and grandparents have the luxury of knowing approximately when the child will arrive. Grandparents can therefore plan to be physically present at the time of birth. Sentimentally, the parent knows that the biological family and the ancestral line will be perpetuated. This is an issue of strong importance to some grandparents, whereas for others it doesn't matter very much.

With adoption, some parents prefer their family to be very involved with the process; others prefer less family involvement. I urge, however, that once the decision to adopt is made and the process has begun, parents can invite grandparents to participate in the happy expectant phase, just the same as is done with a biological child. Just as with a biological child, the arrival date of an adopted child can be unpredictable, often announced by a last-minute phone call after a frustratingly long wait or frequent disappointments. An important difference, though, is the age of the child. Adopted children come in all ages, so the child may not necessarily be a newborn.

Sometimes expectant adoptive parents experience painful disappointments when a child is not delivered as promised or when birth parents have second thoughts about giving up their child and want the child returned. If these glitches occur, share the pain and disappointment with grandparents. They can empathize with the hurt and lend encouragement while the wait continues.

Fortunately, the way a child arrives has little bearing on *how much* the child is loved. Glenna, thirty-seven, an adoptive mother of two, has sisters and brothers with biological children. This makes her own parents, Angelina and Mario, grandparents to both biological and adopted grandchildren. Glenna's parents have gone through the experience of expecting a biological grandchild and an adopted one as well. Angelina said, "With our oldest daughter's first child, we went through the whole thing, getting excited about the pregnancy, the baby showers, buying all kinds of things for the baby, and we even knew the baby was a boy in advance. But it was different when Glenna adopted. She had a bad pelvic infection when she was young, so she couldn't hold a baby. We suffered together with Glenna and her husband through the pregnancy tests and cried with her through two miscarriages and when she accepted that she would never have her own baby. And then there were the long discussions with them about whether to adopt and how we would feel with an adopted grandchild. Then were we in for a surprise! They told us they were going to adopt a one-year-old Chinese baby girl. Mario and I looked at each other. I saw his jaw drop. But they were so happy, we did not question their decision. So we went through the whole deal with them. Best thing we ever did. Now I have a China doll for a granddaughter."

Seeking Biological Parents

Raising any child can be difficult at times, but even more so with an adopted child. When times get rough, a grandparent can be especially helpful to a bedraggled parent. This is especially so when an adopted child is wrestling with the thoughts and feelings that come with being adopted.

Parents of an adopted child are well aware, intellectually, of the need of the child to think about and desire to seek out the birth parents. Dealing with it emotionally is something else. This urge becomes stronger with age and is especially strong for an adolescent who is striving for independence (see the section discussing adolescence later in the chapter). Parents should understand that the need for many adoptees to search out their birth parents should not be taken in any way as a reflection of the child's love and attachment to the adopted parents. It is just that we all need to know our roots.

With technology, such searches are becoming easier to do. Many formerly sealed birth records are now open, offering free and unlimited access to adopted individuals.

As understandable as the child's urge to find the birth parents may be, it is often hard for even the most wonderful parents to deal emotionally with such a search. The mind understands, but the heart hurts. That is when parents can use a loving grandparent to help and to bring perspective to the situation.

Ace, fourteen years old, not wanting to hurt his parents, went to his grandfather to express his wish to search for his biological mother. "My friends know I am adopted, and one of them who is adopted too met his birth parents and said it was great. So I thought about it a lot. Grandpa is a doctor so I spoke to him first. Then I asked him to be there when I spoke to my parents about it. I couldn't have done it alone because I thought I would hurt their feelings, and I knew grandpa would help explain that I didn't want to hurt them."

His mother was grateful to her father for helping Ace bring his feelings to the fore. "I knew he must be wondering about his birth mother, but he never brought up the subject with me or my husband. I guess he thought he would hurt our feelings. He's such a nice kid. I am glad, though, that daddy was there for him. He kept Ace's feelings in the family. Ace sees now that we did not fall apart. He knows it is not easy for us, because we feel so close to him. We are his real parents in every sense of the word, but he knows we accept his need to find out about his origins, and we will all do it together."

Some parents I know have asked grandparents to participate in the search as their proxy, approaching it with the child as a family adventure. Other grandparents provide support by talking with their grandchild after the initial meeting with the birth parents and experience the usual cascade of emotions that the child might find too hard to express to parents at first.

Louise, eighteen, talked "with my grandmother for two days after I met my birth parents. I told her things I could not tell my parents right away. I liked my birth mother and my two half brothers. I did not want to say that to my parents because I did not want them to feel I do not love them. When I was at their house, my mother called to see how I was doing and grammy told her, 'Don't worry, Louise loves you.' After I went home, my mother told me that grammy's comment meant so much to her because mom was so worried about me. She knew what I was going through, and we talked about it, but I had to talk to my grandmother first."

How Grandparents Can Help with Adopted Kids' Growing Pains

Grandparents can be of great help whenever children are having growing pains or are getting themselves in hot water. They can be even more helpful when adopted children are concerned. Biological children are secure in their attachments even when they are feuding with their parents. They know that they are stuck with their parents no matter what! This remains true even if they get mad at their parents and threaten to run away from home. Fortunately, this is not a practical option because there is nowhere for the child to go. As Lee, twelve years old, said, "I have no other parents and no place to go that is not my family. Running away to my grandparents doesn't count."

However, when adopted children are feuding with their parents, the bonds of love and attachment can be very threatened. Even though parent and child might be emotionally close and deeply attached, the fact that a biological link doesn't exist can become a topic of contention, and insecurity, for a child. This makes everyone insecure about the amount of stress that the relationship can take. A fifteen-year-old adopted boy who was pushing his parents once asked me, "Is there a difference between what a parent can take from an adopted child and a biological one?"

When involved in a conflict or crisis situation, both parents and adopted children may report "scary and unwanted thoughts" of regret or second-guessing about having adopted a child or having been adopted. As fleeting as these thoughts are, they can add an extra dose of fear and insecurity to a run-of-the-mill parent-child conflict (about manners, school grades, bedtime, curfew, selection of friends, and so forth). When the stakes are higher (defiance, danger, drugs), grandparent help is needed to defuse the situation and help everyone hold on until it passes: which it eventually does.

In a crisis, adopted children may use the threat of finding birth parents, and living with them, as a bargaining chip to get what they want from parents. As many adoptive parents will attest, there are times in the heat of the fray when a rebellious teenager will test their love and commitment with this litany. At the same time, an adoptive parent may be hard put not to think, "Why do I need to put up with this? You're not my 'real' child. Why did I ever adopt you?"

As Jan, a forty-four-year-old mother with a rebellious fourteen-year-old daughter, put it, "In my heart of hearts, I sometimes think—and I hate myself for it—that maybe I should not have adopted Patty. She is so contrary. She has not said anything nice to me for over a year. The only redeeming feature is that she gets along great with all of her grandparents. They tell me to hang in there, that she will recover from adolescence. My mother and father told me that I was not easy to be around at the same age either."

If children threaten to leave home when they are angry, point them to grandma's house. Fiona, thirty-eight, had a "big fight" with her adopted son, Liam, seventeen, when he came home well past his curfew on a Saturday night. "My husband was away on business; I waited and waited for Liam. He walked in one hour past his curfew. I was so angry at him. . . . he had alcohol on his breath. I lost my temper and told him to get out, that I was ashamed of him.

"He has a real temper too, and he started yelling at me. 'You are not my real mother,' he said. That is something he has been pulling for the last few years when he screws up.

"'Too bad,' I said, 'that doesn't work with me.' He said he had no place to go. I said that I'd drive him to my parents' house because I did not want him at home if he was not going to follow my rules. I called them, woke them up actually, and my father said he would be glad to keep him for the night. I know it wasn't much of a punishment, but Liam got the message. He didn't seem very disturbed about his 'punishment' when he came home the next day, but he's been on time since—more or less."

Guidelines for Grandparents with Adopted Kids

Grandparents are a great asset for having fun and bringing an adopted child into the heart of the family. The adoptive child–grandparent bond can be especially close because it is free of much of the Sturm und Drang that parents experience. So make sure to bring your child and your parents close together. Start from the beginning. Here are some ideas and suggestions to make this happen:

- Include grandparents in all aspects of the adoptive decision process.
- Include grandparents in welcoming your new child.
- Discuss grandparents' feelings about adoption openly and freely.
- Monitor and be aware of *your* feelings.
- Be especially aware of supporting the bond between your child and grandparents.
- Talk with your child about how he experiences grandparents.
- When the inevitable parent-child conflicts arise, use grandparents for advice, emotional support, and respite for your child and for you. After all, your mom can still take you to a movie too.
- Bring your child and grandparents together, and let them do their thing.

Special Needs and Situations

A new child embodies everyone's hopes and dreams: someone to carry on the family culture, to surpass one's own achievements, perhaps to make the world a better place. When a new baby arrives, parents and grandparents expect to greet a healthy child who will bring joy and happiness to the family.

Fortunately, this is what happens most of the time. Even with all the joy and love, rearing any child is no bed of roses. Every child has special needs. Children can sometimes drive us batty, worry us when they fall ill, drag us along as they agonize with growing pains (especially during adolescence), and more. A grandparent's help can be very useful.

When a child has a more serious mental or physical problem or a developmental challenge, a grandparent's help is indispensable. A seriously ill child consumes a loving parent's life, so help from the family team is sorely needed. I will deal with both circumstances in this chapter.

Grandparenting an Adolescent

Let's see how we can use grandparents' help with some "routine miseries" involved in rearing children. I'll use a growing adolescent as an example because grandparents can be especially useful for children at this stage of life. Before I begin, however, let's consider the adolescent "condition."

The average adolescent child is not very emotionally stable. She can be exciting and challenging, interesting and fun, exasperating and lovable, all in the same day (or hour). Along with her growing pains comes a great deal of confusion— especially today when she can be socially bombarded with school pressure and worries about peer acceptance. Often grouchy and seemingly out of sync with life, she has to deal with a changing body, moods, and a confused personal identity, as well as become accustomed to new and powerful feelings. She is now obsessed with her peer group. What do they think about her? Does she fit in? Is she "with it, cool enough?" She must deal with all of this *plus* the added stress of living in a consumer society that places pressures on people for physical and material conformity. The average adolescent stores up this anguish and dumps it on her poor parents. Ideally, the parents have enough time and emotional room to let the misery run off them like water off a duck's back. When they can't, grandparent help is needed.

It's not the adolescent's fault. Teenagers create emotional conflict with us as a side effect of their psychological and emotional growth. Just as a young child strives to be our clone, our teenager hastens in the opposite direction and struggles to be *as different from us as possible*. The adolescent seeks to discover his own identity and establish an independent self by *separating* psychologically and emotionally from us. This can be dangerous if the youngster has no other alternative except a peer group, and especially if the peer group is involved in dangerous activities.

That's why we can use contact with grandparents as a positive alternative, as well as to give us the support (and the break) we need during this trying time. Grandparents have more or less of an "expert status." After all, they survived our own adolescence. Because they have been there and done that, they have the credentials to act as a referee between our child and us. When they tell him what we were like at his age, it will not only be comforting to him, it will also help put things in perspective.

The adolescent sees a grandparent as his parent's own parent—a "higher power" to act on his behalf. Sam, sixteen years old, asked his grandmother to help him convince his parents to allow him to go abroad with a church mission after he graduated from high school. His parents were against it, feeling that Sam was still too young to go so far away. Nevertheless, as Sam reports, "My grandmother gave them a talking-to and told them they were being overprotective. She reminded my father of what he did at my age." Sam's parents decided to let him go.

Using the Special Grandparent Relationship

Our relationship with our child is psychologically and socially different from the child's relationship with grandparents. One reason is that the psychological process of *emotional separation* between parents and adolescent child does not come into play between child and grandparents. The child is not as psychologically entwined with a grandparent as with us. Consequently, the child doesn't see grandparents as the ultimate authority and doesn't need to separate from them to establish an identity. As a result, they don't have much to squabble about. That is why it is easier for our child to follow their rules and comply with their wishes. After all, no laws, no criminals.

Grandparents don't threaten our child very much because the child perceives them as weaker than us. An adolescent can therefore ally himself with grandparents and use them as a source of stability—an *emotional sanctuary* from the world. Unfortunately, when a grandparent is the primary caregiver for the child, these dynamics are very different.

When it comes to an adolescent's life-quality issues (such as obtaining a good education) or life-threatening issues (such as safe driving, behavior, alcohol, and drugs), it is important that we develop a family policy and expect grandparents to support our policy. It is especially important to provide our adolescent respite from any *external stresses* that we as adults might be suffering. And this is even more important when circumstances consume a great deal of personal time and attention (divorce, parental remarriages, mental illness, family financial instability, and so forth). Some teenagers handle stressful life changes more smoothly, whereas others may need to be guided and supported through these times. Ideally, a three-dimensional support team composed of healthy, loving, available parents and stable, understanding grandparents can supply the emotional bedrock on which a stressed-out teenager can rely.

In emergencies, we can use grandparents as an emergency response team (our "EMTs"). We should be especially alert to any severe emotional or behavioral changes in our child that may be a symptom of something more serious—for example, a drop in school grades, blatant drug use, depression, or eating disorders. If a child does become chemically dependent or abuse drugs, a family intervention with grandparents can help greatly. It is always helpful for any acting-out teenager to see that all of the family cares.

Teenagers have many questions about commonplace issues, especially sex and romance. Make sure to be clear with grandparents about your feelings concerning the "big" issues, such as the "facts of life" (although most children today seem to be fully versed on the topic). Undoubtedly, our child will be talking about sex with her peers, but she will want to hear from us and everyone else too—especially when it concerns romance! Sharing our intimate personal stories about how we met a lover or spouse and what our first date was like are not just lessons to learn. This is the stuff of legend—family histories that she will one day pass on to her own children, our grandchildren. The personal stories that we and our parents share with our child will help her gain some perspective on life. She will realize that although she and her friends are currently struggling through developmental hard times, people have been struggling with these same issues, and worse, since time immemorial. Even parents!

So get grandparents involved in the world of your teenage child—nose rings and all. Take Alice, forty-three, for example. Alice got her own mother involved in her teen daughter's world. When her daughter, Claire, started peppering her with questions about love, sex, and romance, Alice asked her own mother, Cecile, seventy-three, to "check out Claire's life." So Cecile, who lives nearby, started a weekly get-together with Claire and her friends.

Soon Cecile became "one of the girls." "The girls are all around sixteen. They like to hear about the old days, what it was like when I was courting: 'old-fashioned sex,' as they call it. To tell the truth, I have learned a thing or two myself. Sometimes I hear things that make my ears red! They are exposed to so much so early. All that sex. And the drugs! Why, back then, we didn't even know that stuff existed. The sad thing is one of their friends became pregnant at the age of fifteen. She dropped out of school and then gave the baby up for adoption. She is back in school now, but that sure scared the rest of the girls. I just try to keep an open mind and not judge, that's all." Alice was pleased, so was Claire.

"I am proud of my grandma," Claire said. "She doesn't look down on us, and she's interested in what we are doing. I can talk to her about lots of stuff, like this boy I like at school. I could never talk to my mom or dad about that. My friends are all jealous of me because I have a cool grandma."

Grandparents can be our greatest ally in raising a teenager. Call on them to make things happier, relieve any burdens, and help in adversity. That is what being a three-dimensional parent is all about. Remember, our child is watching and learning.

Helping with Illness or Disability

Some children experience more serious, often life-threatening, issues. Whenever a child has a serious mental or physical illness or disability, that child's emotional and physical needs are intense, especially when ongoing care is indicated. A child's illness places a great burden on parents and can often be overwhelming. That's when grandparents can help their child and grandchild.

Grandparents' ability to help most effectively can be improved when they are educated and included in all aspects of the healing or remedial process. Asking grandparents for help might not come to mind when a child's illness is first discovered. There are several reasons for this. When a child has a mental illness or a developmental disability, most of us have a tendency to first minimize—or even deny—the condition. Then there is the reflex to blame oneself (or some grandparents to blame parents) for the problem. Fortunately, recent changes in accepting such disabling, or challenging, conditions have made it easier for us to ask for help.

For a heartwarming example of what I mean, attend a Special Olympics competition. By working together as members of a family team, parents and grandparents can help one another accept the reality of having an ill or challenged child and can handle it in a positive way. With thorough education, understanding, compassion, and the appropriate sharing of tasks, we can ensure that our challenged child's spirit flourishes and that the best possible medical outcome is achieved.

I have made it a point to urge parents with an ill or developmentally challenged child to ask grandparents (and stepgrandparents) to get involved as soon as possible. The healthy spirit of any child with special needs (no matter what the problem is) wants to love and be loved, to grow, to learn, to have freedom, and to have fun to the best of his ability. Grandparents can supplement our own efforts to fill this need. Although we have the primary responsibility for following medical regimens and giving direct care, we need grandparents as backups, to supplement our efforts, offer us respite, and give us a pat on the back when needed.

When parents suffer, grandparents suffer as well. Expect, therefore, that a grandparent's ability to help may be affected by the grandparent's own emotional reactions to a suffering or ill child. So as much as they can help us, we may have to help *them* sort through their own grief, thoughts, and feelings about the child's condition. Just as we do, grandparents may enter a state of denial or may even be embarrassed at first about a child's condition. One grandmother that I know initially felt embarrassed when she took her moderately retarded granddaughter with Down's syndrome to a public playground. "I was ashamed of myself for feeling embarrassed at first. Seeing my granddaughter with all those other children and how different she is made me feel self-conscious. But I soon got over that. Now we go everywhere together. She is such a sweetie."

Some grandparents, in their anguish, may even blame parents for the child's condition until they know more about the problem. That's why it is so important to include grandparents in every step of a child's medical evaluation and treatment. There is not enough space here to discuss each one of the many varieties of mental and physical conditions that can affect children and how families react specifically to each condition. Instead I will present, in a case example, helpful information that may be applied to address any condition a child may have (mental retardation, cerebral palsy, diabetes, heart disease, and so forth).

This example illustrates what parents and grandparents experience when a child has a problem and how they can satisfactorily coordinate their helping efforts. I will use *attention deficit disorder* (ADD)—a common condition of children that stresses parents greatly and often causes perceptual and attitudinal differences between parents and grandparents—as an example.

Attention deficit disorder affects approximately one out of twelve children and five boys for every girl. It can be present with or without hyperactivity. It is a confusing malady to the family because, most often, the child looks fine and healthy but behaves in an impulsive way, often sporadically, and unpredictably. For example, a child with ADD who is visiting a zoo or watching a favorite television program might seem to behave as well as any other child.

But ask the child to pay attention to something that requires prolonged concentration, especially in a subject in which he is not interested, and symptoms appear. Although usually quite intelligent, the child has trouble with concentrating, paying attention, and controlling behavior on request. This bewilders not only the confused youngster (who does not want to act in such a manner) but everyone else as well—especially the child's parents. Grandparents may think that the beleaguered parents are exacerbating—if not causing—the child's problems. They can upset parents even more by offering useless suggestions that don't work. It is therefore common for ADD to cause conflicts between both parents, as well as between parents and grandparents. When untreated, this condition not only can seriously impair the child but can create a great deal of marital and family turmoil as well.

Of all the illnesses I have treated over the years, ADD is one of the most subtle and difficult because often the child does not appear to be ill. In other illnesses or conditions—diabetes, mental retardation, leukemia—the child is obviously ill and suffering. Not so with ADD. That is why a great deal of maturity and compassion is necessary to deal successfully with an ADD child. If you have an ADD child, getting grandparents involved may require a major effort on your part. However, as you will see, when you do, it is worth it.

Here is one example of how, through the parents' efforts, a grandfather came to understand the parents and help them more effectively with an ADD child. His earlier mistakes, and his successful comeback, serve as a model of compassion, understanding, and self-examination that we all should strive to emulate. Here is an edited version of a letter that he wrote to the parents, chronicling the journey of learning that he and his wife have undertaken. I include some of my own comments in italics in the body of the letter.

Dear Kids (you are still kids to us),

This letter is not easy to write but here goes. A lot has happened since our grandchild was born. We remember the worry and nervousness that go along with any birth, the fear of the birth defects, the unknown . . . then the burst of joy when everything seemed to be OK. Our expectations and hopes soared with you, as our grandchild appeared to be free of problems and ready to thrive in this world. We remember starting to watch you raise your child, and we gave our advice generously, basing it on the wisdom we had gained from raising you. You turned out fine, which proves that we are experts! Then as your child grew and started to present problems that you could not solve, despite our ever-so-helpful advice, we thought to ourselves that YOU must be doing something wrong. (*They were becoming judgmental—blaming the parents.*) Both you, and we, his grandparents, were caught unprepared for the scenario that began to unfold before our eyes.

Behavioral patterns seen only in "other families" became a very real tragedy for you and were completely misunderstood by us. We muttered in the background, "If only they would . . . Whose genes? . . . Not mine, for sure! Why do they indulge him? Nothing is wrong when he is with us! . . . A good old-fashioned spanking!" (*This expresses a vast array of emotions that a child's problem elicits in all adults—anger, frustration, social embarrassment, and more. It illustrates again how sometimes parents and grandparents can "blame" one another for a child's problem.*)

As our advice developed an edge, we were unknowingly joining the chorus that accompanied you as you moved through your daily routines with your child. (*Here they are moving away from and being critical of a parent who is trying to do her best and needing their support.*) You felt blamed from all directions. People in stores glared at you as you tried, over and over, to get your child to behave. You were constantly embarrassed by being "obviously" bad at parenting, unable to put our infallible advice to use.

The next bitter pill came when you let it be known that you were seeking professional help, not only for your child but also for yourself. To us, who had based our philosophies of life upon self-reliance and religious principles, you may as well have signed up with a witch doctor! We felt you were rejecting our tried-and-true ways and were about to be exploited by false experts, who spouted mysterious labels: "Oppositional?" "ADD?" "ADHD?" "LD?" "Fine and gross motor delay?" and other mumbo jumbo, who would take advantage of your gullibility, take your money, and do no good. We let you know of our misgivings, but we had gotten used to your weary voices and eyes, telling us, in response to our objections, what your so-called experts were telling you.

Thank God there was enough love in our family to weather those awful times, when we actually added to your burden. And thank God you listened to the experts! Finally, after years of heartbreak, all that mumbo jumbo started to make sense. (*Now their education starts, and they are moving toward the parents.*) Gradually, we began to see that our grandchild was not just a spoiled brat. We began to recognize patterns in his behavior, which were, at last, understandable to us, based upon principles promoted by your experts. We became more familiar with the jargon, as we tentatively entered what was, for us, foreign and uncharted territory. We, who thought we were educated, experienced, and tough, are babes in the woods compared to you, you KIDS, who are now able to teach us. Now we can listen to you and HEAR you. (*Here they are becoming understanding and reestablishing the family team.*)

Although we have felt all along that we are in the same boat, now all of our oars are pulling in the same direction. It is still a rugged journey, but we hope it is a little easier now that we aren't sniping at you. So kids, please forgive us. We hope we can heal the hurt brought about by our misunderstanding of our struggle. Our hearts are filled with love and the best of intentions for you and our grandchild. We are your flesh and blood. We want so much to help that we pray that our clumsy efforts can provide some measure of comfort and support for you all! Thanks for hanging in there, until you could reach us and teach us. One thing we have learned: you are GOOD parents for our grandchild, the best. He needs you.

And now let us preach a little. We are lucky. We are bonded together by love, strengthened by the trials that could have fractured a less-fortunate family. Thanks to that love, we have a unified family-support group that will not waver, essential if our grandchild is to have a solid foundation upon which to build his life. We will always be here for you, if you should ever need an ear, a shoulder, or, God forbid, advice! That is what grandparents are for!

Love, Dad[1]

This letter clearly documents the developing process of this grandfather's experience with his grandchild who has special needs. Knowing how this emotional process unfolds in both parents and grandparents can help you recognize where grandparents are in this cycle. With this knowledge, you can communicate with them and use them more effectively. Here is a brief summary of what families experience, and what they need to do, for a child with special needs:

- *Initial shock, denial, disbelief.* There is emotional pain and confusion upon discovery that a child has an illness or disability. The disappointment is worsened because of the contrast with the initial joy experienced with having the child.

- *Blame and disappointment.* Often, even if grandparents are supportive, parents will feel guilty, defensive, and some even ashamed about their child's condition. Grandparents may initially feel the same way.

- *Sadness, even depression, hopelessness and despair.* Many parents hit bottom at this point and need maximum support. This is when they need to ask grandparents for help.

- *Acceptance.* At some point, acceptance begins to occur. When this happens, the pain and disappointment start to wane.

- *Reality.* When reality sets in, the family can then go about determining what can be done about the child's condition and

then decide to get to work. This is an optimum time to activate grandparents' efforts.

- *Action*. During this phase, the family begins to take positive
  steps to do the best for the child. This is when the parents
  take over.

- *Family team*. Under the parents' direction, the family works
  together to develop and implement the necessary remedial
  plan. This last phase is tailored to the form and location of
  family members. Although long-distance grandparents may
  only be periodically available, they can help financially or
  by keeping up-to-date with the latest information concerning
  the child's condition. Frequent visiting should be encouraged.

- *Parents' needing a break*. Planning for such respite is very
  important. Parents can recruit grandparents' assistance by
  asking the grandparents to take the child in their home for a
  while or baby-sit while the parents get away for needed rest.

Preparing to Ask

Here are some ideas and suggestions for parents regarding their own
soul-searching and what to do even before they ask grandparents for
help. This is important because grandparents will need to follow the
parent's directions as leader of the therapeutic team.

- Understand your own feelings about your child's condition.

- Talk to your spouse, a friend, or grandparents. You need support too.

- Establish a methodology for what you and your child need—a
  therapeutic plan.

- Determine what grandparents can do to help: make them part
  of the plan.

- Educate the grandparents about your child's condition. Take
  them to visit the doctor, if appropriate, to help them understand both the condition and the treatment process.

- Formulate a cooperative family policy on helping. For example, grandparents can help with time and money.

Be vigilant about the state of the family's mental and physical health. It is unfortunate but true that when people are faced with difficult external stresses, there is often a tendency to turn on one another, to be judgmental, and to become critical and angry. This adds to the hurt that everyone is feeling. Do not let that happen.

Dealing with Divorce

Every divorced person is aware of the stress involved in the breakup of a family, and especially the toll on children. A child sees a divorced parent through an emotional kaleidoscope—the parent appears wounded, confused, angry, hurt, sad, and more. If you are divorced, your child is aware of your suffering, and (depending on her age) she will share her feelings with you in just the amount she thinks you can bear. In other words, because your child is frightened and depends on you for her life, she will tell you what she thinks you want to hear and just enough so you aren't overwhelmed.

How much emotion, and what kind of emotion, a child feels depends on the circumstances of the divorce. Here is where you can ask grandparents for help. Your child will feel a lot easier sparing you and sharing her feelings with a close grandparent. By lending a sympathetic ear and allowing the child to vent her feelings, grandparents can help you ease your child's distress and assure you that your child is cared for. To a child in turmoil, the love and support of a grandparent in such circumstances is enormously reassuring.

As Emery, eleven, said during his parents' very acrimonious divorce, "My parents are there and sometimes they are not. Even when they are there, it is hard to get their attention because they are so unhappy. But my grandparents are always there. They have the time to listen to me without interrupting. It's especially good because they don't say anything bad about either of my parents. If they did that, I couldn't talk with them."

Stages of Children's Reactions to Divorce

The emotional repercussions of divorce occur in stages. Parents can call on grandparents to help a child at different stages. To do so, it is important to become familiar with exactly what emotional stages children go through in the divorce. Here are some classic examples to illustrate this point, which you can use to educate grandparents who want to help.

1. *Sadness and bewilderment.* Reggie, ten years old, is in a sad mood about his parents' divorce. "I feel so sad. I tell myself that my parents will always love me no matter what, but it is so sad. I feel like my old life is gone. I was happy before mom and dad started fighting. I still love them, but they don't love each other anymore. Since I come from both of them, what does that mean I am? When I am with my grandparents, I feel like it is the old family time."

2. *Fear and anger.* Ramon, nine years old, feels strong emotions of fear, anger, and insecurity. "My parents don't want to be together. If I was not alive, they probably would not have to talk to each other. I am angry at them, and I make trouble on purpose to get back at them. I know I am doing it too. My grandparents are like my parents now because they are together, and I love them and am important to them. I never make trouble for them. I know they care for my parents and me. I feel safe when I am with them and know I can always live with them if something happens."

3. *Guilt.* Children may feel guilty and have thoughts of personal responsibility for their parents' divorce. Children need to be reassured that the divorce is not their fault and that everybody loves them. Angel, fourteen years old, feels, like so many other children, an irrational sense of responsibility for her parents' divorce.

   "I know they fought over me sometimes. My mother would protect me when my father was drunk or high and would be affectionate, not in any bad way. Then they would fight. Sometimes I think that maybe if it weren't for me, they'd still be together. My mother asked my grandparents to talk with me. They said I should not feel guilty because it's a normal feeling. 'Divorce happens,' my grandma said. 'It's a grown-up thing and has nothing to do with kids.'"

4. *Anxiety and depression*. All of the emotions just described are often accompanied by anxiety and depression. In children, this anxiety is manifested by nervousness and by feelings of panic and impending doom; some even have difficulty breathing. Sometimes a child will experience anxiety in brief yet intense "attacks." In other instances, a child may experience low-level anxiety. The longer the anxiety continues, the more a child will become increasingly depressed.

The signs of depression are rather easy to identify. The child's functioning is affected. This is manifested by a lack of attention, depressed mood, lethargy, a negative attitude, irritability, and the verbal expression of feelings such as helplessness, hopelessness, and worthlessness. Conversely, the child may act out and become a behavior problem. Sometimes children think they can bring their parents together by getting sick or doing something self-destructive. With more severe depression, sleep and eating patterns become chaotic, and suicidal thoughts enter the child's mind. If you notice any of these symptoms, gather the family team and seek professional help for your child.

Peebee, ten years old, "got sick to my stomach when dad left the house after a big fight and said he wanted a divorce, and he couldn't put up with us anymore." For days afterward, Peebee stayed in bed, sobbing and angry. She refused to go to school or to talk to her friends.

Her mother was "beside myself with worry." She called on her own parents to intervene. Peebee's grandmother said that she would stay in the room with Peebee until she felt better. Her grandmother sat up all night next to Peebee's bed. The next day, her grandmother stayed in the chair and said she was staying right there until Peebee was well. By that evening, Peebee began to improve. When she was asked why she was out of bed, she said that she was worried about her grandmother's health and knew that her grandmother would not leave Peebee until she got better.

What to Ask Grandparents to Do

The first things a divorced parent should ask grandparents to do are to offer the child respite from any parental conflict, focus the child's mind elsewhere, and above all try to have some fun.

Sal, twelve years old, is pleased that his grandparents do not put him in the middle of family conflicts. "My parents criticize each other all of the time. My grandparents used to criticize them too. Now if my grandparents criticize my parent who is their own child, it is OK. But they shouldn't criticize my other parent, especially to me, because it makes me upset. I would rather not hear about the differences the grown-ups have. When my grandparents criticized my parents, it made me more upset. Grandparents should help parents instead of criticizing them. What good does criticizing do?"

Upon hearing Sal's feelings, his grandparents stopped criticizing anyone. Now Sal says, "Now I get to criticize my parents to my grandparents, and they say they won't rat on me. My parents say I am always more relaxed after I come back from my grandparents' house. And of course, I have a lot of fun with my grandparents too." When the emotional turmoil from the divorce recedes a bit, grandparents can help parents get their lives back on track. One way is to take care of the child while the parent begins dating or gets together with a new partner.

Assistance in Coping with a Parent's Dating and Remarriage

Eventually, most divorced people date, find a new partner, and remarry or cohabit. Often this can be very hard for children to deal with. When this is the case, I recommend that parents increase their child's time with grandparents while the parents tend to their social lives. When divorced parents date, children need people to fill their time. Otherwise they become fearful of losing a socially busy parent's attention, while at the same time having to deal with a new person (whom they don't particularly want to be there) in the parent's life, at a very vulnerable time.

You need to keep your love life separate from parenting, so if you are in such a situation, ask grandparents to care for your child when you date. Lillet, twelve years old, is upset that her mother started dating again and explains what she feels: "One thing grandparents can do is give advice about the kind of person a divorced parent wants to date. Parents don't realize that children are frightened when their parents get divorced and then start dating other people. That new person might turn into the new stepparent and that can scare a kid, especially if they don't like that person. And then they have to pretend they like the person, or their parent will get upset. I can complain to my grandparents about who my mother goes out with, and they listen to me. Sometimes they talk to my mom about it too . . . even though I know she does not want to hear it. I like it when my grandparents help my mom."

Grandparents can also help a grandchild adjust when a parent remarries and can give the new couple some time to adjust. Some grandparents that I know took their grandchildren into their home to allow the newlyweds to spend some time together. Lending an ear so a grandchild can express feelings about a new stepparent is very helpful too. If you are remarried, allowing your child to spend time with grandparents and to get to know the new spouse in a slow and relaxed manner is the best prescription for minimizing conflicts.

Grandparents as Mediators

If conflicts arise between you and your child because of your divorce, ask grandparents for help. Because children see their grandparents as their own "parents' parents" (having a similar power and authority over the parents as the parents do over the child), it makes sense for them to try to use grandparents to wield some degree of power and influence over their parents.

So when a family problem exists, it is natural for a child to turn to a grandparent for help. Because the grandparent may not be directly involved in the problem, the child can feel safe expressing feelings and opinions about his own parent, in confidence, to a grandparent.

Bill, forty-seven, was "tired of listening to my sons trash me because I left their mother. They just wouldn't listen to my side of the story at all. I was the bad guy and that's it." Bill was very upset about being rejected by his sons and went to his own mother for advice. She told him that she would talk to the boys. It took awhile, but eventually grandma got through, and Bill reconciled with his sons.

Fred, twenty-two, Bill's older son, said, "I couldn't face my father because I was so mad at him. But grandma was able to explain what happened and why, in a way I could understand. Now I am trying to make the best of it."

After the Divorce

Grandparents can be helpful in managing the postdivorce logistics. A single, newly divorced parent needs time to adjust and accommodate to the changes. For example, a father's ex-wife may have custody of the children, so his visitation may be limited. He can call on his own parents to help keep contact with the children and maintain family continuity. That's what Red, thirty-nine, did after his divorce. "Since I drive a truck for a living, I am gone a lot of the time. Therefore I ask my folks to put in my time for me with the children. They are happy to do it, and my ex-wife is happy too. She's really pissed off at me, but she gets along with my folks."

Like some parents who are newly divorced, you may want to move in lock, stock, and barrel to your parents' home for a while. Your child will be especially sensitive to how you get along with your parents. If you need to exercise such an option, be sure to discuss the length of the stay, financial terms, household responsibilities, baby-sitting arrangements, parenting and grandparenting responsibilities, private time, and so forth well in advance. And let your child know the rules too.

Grandparents and the Divorce Agreement

If you are contemplating divorce or are already divorced, consider adding a clause to the divorce agreement stating (whether or not you have custody) that your own parents have visiting privileges with your child. Experience has shown that most children stay with the mother after a divorce. This often decreases time with the father, and especially with the grandparents on the father's side of the family. When anger and conflict persist, it becomes easy for one parent or another to exploit the children as pawns in any adult battle. One of the most common casualties in such a battle is the grandparent-grandchild relationship on the side of the noncustodial parent.

Paying attention to grandparents in any divorce agreement sends a wonderful message to children that the third dimension of their family is still intact—and honored—even though their parents have separated. When you do this, however, make it clear to the grandparents that they are expected to be respectful of your feelings at all times, coordinate activities with you, keep the children free from adult conflicts, and act in the best interest of all family members. This is best done via a family conference, where these matters can be openly discussed.

If you are divorced or thinking about getting divorced, get grandparents involved immediately. Foster the relationship between them and your child so that they are close. The closer they are to your child, the more help they can offer, and the more you and your child can benefit. Here are some other ideas and suggestions to help:

- First, acknowledge, evaluate, and work through your own feelings about the divorce.

- Handle the feelings that come up in an appropriate and healthy manner.

- Keep the children as free as possible from the adult turmoil.

- Get grandparents involved.

- Call a family conference with them to hammer out a plan for them to help.

- Reevaluate how you are all doing on a regular basis and adjust your planning accordingly.

Divorce is a painful and complex affair. The grandparents' role is to help you limit the damage and be as supportive as possible. They can bring some fun and joy into your child's life while you rebuild your own life.

When Grandparents Raise Your Child

It is not unusual today for a parent to ask grandparents to raise a child for a period of time. Although there is nothing historically new about this, it is becoming a more frequent occurrence. One recent report from the U.S. Census (which only partially reflects the widespread nature of this issue) made the following comparison: in the year 1970, 2,214,000 children under eighteen lived in grandparent-headed households, with the mother present in half of these households. By the year 1997, the number was reported as 5,435,000, or 7.7 percent, of all children in the United States.[2]

The majority of these children are being raised by two grandparents, or a grandmother alone, with different degrees of parental involvement. Since 1997, the number has increased substantially. In families that have both grandparents and grandchildren, the grandparents are the head of the house three-quarters of the time. The parents are heads of the household in the remaining one-fourth of the homes. In the former arrangement, half of the families have a grandmother and grandfather present. The rest have a grandmother with no spouse. Although official census estimates made in the year 2000 hint that the number could be more than six million, that does not present the full picture. I estimate that the number of children being raised by grandparents in America today, part- or full-time, is now *close to eight million*.

When parents falter (for whatever reason), nature has prearranged it so children naturally fall into the laps of their grandparents. Remember the diagram of the family in the Introduction? Having grandparents care for a child may be temporarily necessary—for example, when a parent is ill or in turmoil. It can also be a permanent arrangement, in the case of parental death, chronic illness, serious substance abuse, or incarceration. Some of the most frequent reasons for parents' asking grandparents to raise their child are abandonment of the child by the parent, parental illness (mental or physical), teenage pregnancy, substance abuse, unemployment, homelessness, incarceration, death of a parent, divorce, family violence, child abuse and neglect, and poverty.

If you need grandparents to raise your child, be alert to the difficulties inherent in the arrangement. When grandparents raise a child, it puts a strain on generational boundaries. The difficult and tricky task that grandparents face is to keep their grandparent identity while acting in the parent's place. My experience (and that of others) shows that children raised by grandparents always hope and dream that their parents will return and care for them one day.[3] They also would prefer their grandparents to remain grandparents.

Even in the worst-case scenario, when a parent abandons a child, the child cannot banish a parent from his mind and heart. A parent is a parent forever. Children who lose their parents create dreams and fantasies to deal with the loss, such as idealizing their parents, having fantasies of being reunited with them, and the like. Just as they may project anger onto a custodial parent because of the pain of divorce, children may rationalize the loss of parents and even blame grandparents for their loss. Parents must therefore alert grandparents not to cross generational boundaries between the child and the parent. Grandparents have to be flexible in replacing a parent's functions as needed by the child. They need to learn how to move in and out of their roles as nurturer, mentor, role model, playmate, and GRANDparent.

This point is demonstrated by the example of a grandmother who asked her granddaughter that she raises, Paula, eight, "Do you want me to be your grandmother acting like a parent, or should I just be your mother?"

Paula (whose parents had died) replied, "If I am your grandchild, then I am not someone's 'child' and have no mother or father. And if I don't have you as a mother, I don't have anybody. So I want you to be my mother, not my grandmother." When her grandmother signed the custody papers, Paula said, "Gramma, when I go to school tomorrow, can I tell them I have a real mom now? But I will call you gramma at home." Clearly, Paula needed her grandmother to play the role of parent. As Paula ages, her feelings may change, or perhaps she will always need to see her grandmother in the guise of a parent.

What Children Feel

If you have to place your child in a grandparent's care for a protracted period, let the child know the reasons for your decision. Depending on the circumstances, the child will be more or less accepting of your choice. When death or severe illness or incarceration is the reason, children tend to understand more readily. When it is an arbitrary decision or appears to be such, children can have problems accepting the situation.

When Carrie, twelve, found out that both of her parents (who were in the U.S. Foreign Service) had to go overseas to a dangerous posting, she was upset that she would have be in the care of her grandparents, and without her parents, for two years. She became so heartsick that her mother had to resign her job and stay home with her. In contrast, Rod, nine years old, who doesn't know his father, was relieved when the court arranged for him to live with his grandmother after his mother had been sentenced to prison for drug dealing and robbery.

It should be of comfort to any parent to know that studies show that children without serious preexisting problems can be better adjusted when raised by grandparents than many children in single parent or remarried families are. They can also have fewer behavioral problems and be better adapted socially. But studies acknowledge that many children do have problems that started before their grandparents took over. In that case, as well intentioned as the grandparent may be, the problems still need to be addressed.

In the long run, be assured that your child is thankful for what grandparents do. Most grandparents realize the importance of what they are doing as well: being quite aware that they are saving their grandchild. Few have reservations about what they have given up to achieve this. Children appreciate their efforts. Walter, seven years old, whose single mother was dying of leukemia, put it well: "If my grandparents didn't take care of me, I'd be dead."

Showing Grandparents Appreciation

Remind grandparents who may be raising your child that they are still your parents as well. No matter how they feel about the circumstances that led you to ask them for help, it's important that they leave a place open for you in their heart. They also have to be able to relinquish parenting to you when your circumstances change for the better, and you are able to resume your parenting role. Whatever the situation is that makes it necessary to ask your parents to raise your child, from the best to the worst of possibilities, always keep the lines of communication open.

Make an effort to understand the grandparents' feelings as well. Depending on the circumstances, some grandparents may resent being asked to care for a grandchild when there are other options— or when they have no say in the matter.

Take Beadie, sixty-two, for example, who woke up one morning to find that her drug-addicted daughter had left her two-year-old on Beadie's doorstep. "I have no choice," she said. "I have to raise this child until my daughter gets better, but the way she is going, I believe I have this little one for life."

Be ready to listen to their resentment for having such a great responsibility thrust on them. Also listen when grandparents may feel that they have failed their own child, who is forced to ask them for help. Ali, sixty-five, said that he must have done something wrong for his son "to turn out like this . . . be such a failure, so much his wife up and left him with three kids he can't support, and my wife and I have to do it."

Make sure to be appreciative and respectful of the fact that the lives of grandparents undergo great change when they take on the care of a grandchild. Instead of spending time with their friends, they become immersed in a younger world—the social life and schoolwork of the child (which also has many advantages). It is important to mention that it can be especially difficult if the child has emotional or behavioral difficulties. If you have to ask grandparents to raise your child for a while, here are some ideas and suggestions that you can use to ease the burden:

- Make sure grandparents have all the necessary medical and legal authorizations.

- Clear your arrangement with school authorities. Many schools will not admit a child unless the child's parent is living with the grandparent; consequently, grandparents are denied authority concerning the schooling of their grandchildren and even transportation to another school district.

- Check for the availability of financial assistance. Social security benefits are not payable to caregiving grandparents unless they adopt the child.

- Check on housing arrangements. The households of caretaking grandparents do not conform to the traditional definition of *family* as defined in zoning laws. As a result, they may be excluded from living in a single family–zoned community.

- Make sure to take advantage of the national organizations that help grandparents who raise grandchildren (see Resources).

Long-Distance Connections

One of the hardest challenges that we face is keeping a family relationship close and meaningful while living far apart from one another. This is especially relevant when it concerns grandparents. Many grandparents today are long-distance grandparents. They do not live close to their children or grandchildren. Some might live near to some of their grandchildren and not to others. As a result, what we can ask of them when we need help is limited by the degree of distance between us.

In spite of these restrictions, we can still access grandparents for help across the miles. Of course, we can ask them to visit or can visit them when needed for hands-on help, or we can travel together. Many varieties of help—financial, verbal support, advice, and more—can be accessed over the phone or through e-mail. It's not like directly asking grandma to soothe a fevered brow, but it's better than nothing. In the past, the "out of sight is out of mind" philosophy was appropriate as far as grandparents being part of daily family life. Not so any longer. Technology has revolutionized our ability to stay in touch on a daily basis in spite of long distances.

The computer is a modern miracle, allowing us to learn, grow, and communicate with one another and the wider world more fully than ever before. Thanks to technology, the reach of family members is now extended beyond the constraints of physical closeness. The latest advances in technology now allow us to maintain a real-time relationship with one another in cyberspace. This is a revolutionary and unexpected blessing for family members that live far from one another. This means that when we need help with a recipe, some advice, a laugh, or just conversation with a long-distance grandparent, we can boot up our computer and get together.

We need to make use of this gift and encourage our child to stay in touch with long-distance grandparents. Millions of what I call *cybergrandparents* are now able to be a daily part of their grandchildren's lives, regardless of where they are geographically located. Cybergrandparents converse with family members via e-mail, help their grandchildren with their homework, participate in family chat lines, play games together, publish family newsletters, research and share their family history, and maintain contact with family members all over the country.

And now with videoconferencing, people can talk to one another face-to-face. Many parents I know keep long-distance grandparents updated by sending weekly pictures of their grandchild. One grandmother I know serves as a self-appointed "research assistant," surfing the Web to help her college student granddaughter with her term papers. Family members who are interested in computers find that they communicate with one another more frequently than other families. Some parents that I know go on-line and shop simultaneously with grandparents, selecting the right dress or carriage for a new child.

Refresh the Bonds as Often as Possible

The problem with distance is that it limits personal contact. And long-distance relationships need personal contact to keep them alive. That is why it is important for us to make sure that personal contact takes place between family members as often as possible. I feel so strongly about this that I advise families to pool their funds to allow long-distance relatives to get together as much as possible. Planning visits for a helping purpose is very important (for example, when parents want to go off on a vacation together and need grandparents to baby-sit). Visits for enjoyment, rites of passage, and celebrations (attending a graduation or a granddaughter's first ballet recital) are important as well.

If grandparents cannot come to us, we can send our child to them (age appropriately, of course). Depending on the child's age, we can accompany the child or not. There is much we can do to maintain continuity between a long-distance grandparent and our child between the times we spend together in person. The principles involved are to maintain continuity and to have the long-distance grandparent be as much a part of the child's daily life as possible under the circumstances. The following are some ideas and suggestions to help:

- When distance becomes a problem, call a family meeting to discuss how all of you can maintain a family team over distance. Hammer out strategies to meet the challenges.

- Because the effects of distance can be mitigated by making frequent contact a family priority, start a family account to finance travel for grandparents and grandchildren. The account can be funded proportionately to the family's income or financial resources.

- It is especially important for long-distance grandparents to be present when a new baby comes along. Make sure there is adequate planning time to make this happen.

- Make a plan to minimize the separation by keeping in constant communication. This is where e-mail, faxes, letters, and phone calls come in.

- Make it a point for grandparents to attend major events and celebrations (family, school, religious, and so forth).

- Have a yearly family reunion.

- Most important, keep up with the technology advances that your family can use to keep together over distance.

When you ask grandparents for help, and they respond in a willing and loving way, you will derive the benefits of creating a family team and managing it as a three-dimensional parent. The examples and guidelines that I have supplied will help you tailor-make your own family team, enhance your present assets, resolve any conflicts, and set the example for three-generational parenting for the next generation and all to come after.

Epilogue: The Four-Dimensional Family

I hope that you too will become a grandparent in your time. Everything you have done and have learned as a three-dimensional parent will equip you to be an effective and powerful presence on your family team. Every joy you have experienced with your own parents, and every conflict you have suffered and resolved with them, are invaluable. All you have experienced to date will make it easier to deal with similar issues with your own child when the time comes that you take your place on the other side of the parent-grandparent equation.

The Vital Future of the Family Team

There is more. Chances are, these days—if you started having kids young and your own children did so as well, and if you're in good health and take good care of yourself—you may become a great-grandparent as well. If this happens, you will find yourself on the leading edge of a *four-dimensional family*. If you become a great-grandparent, you will belong to the first generation of vital, involved, and pioneering great-grandparents to live on this planet. Because this is an unprecedented event, there is no cut-and-dried blueprint for how to live this role or what to do with it.

I speculate that the new great-grandparent will embody some of the characteristics of grandparents of the past, with added wisdom, experience, and power linked to a four-dimensional family perspective. Great-grandparents in the future will become "super" living ancestors and family icons—a presence at family celebrations and rituals, available for love and counsel to all descendants—while exponentially increasing their more passive and mystical roles. The closer they get to heaven, the more their range of influence will increase within the family. Their contribution to the family team will result in a deeper level of love, commitment, meaning, and understanding for everyone in the family and will result in increased and well-deserved respect from their juniors. Perhaps we are on the brink of seeing a race of truly selfless wise men and women—old, seasoned, experienced, and influential. This will be very beneficial for children and will offer future parents another level of love and support.

Great-grandparents of the future move us one step closer to demonstrating on this earth the truth that parenting is truly forever. And you may well write the book on it.

Perhaps it will be the great-grandparents of the future, who started by being three-dimensional parents, who will show the way. The aphorism "we don't get older, we just get better" isn't far from wrong.

When a Grandparent Dies

Death is a teacher.

When a grandparent dies, a parent dies too. That becomes a problem for many grandchildren, because they are not only personally upset at their loss, they are equally upset about their parents' grief. When this happens, as parents, we can easily be so overcome with our own loss that we have no time or energy to pay attention to what our child, the grandchild, goes through.

"When my grandmother died, my parents' mourning was public," said Tina, thirty-two, "and mine was private. When I came home from summer camp—I was twelve at the time—I noticed all of the grown-ups crying. I ran up to my grandmother's room to see her. But she had just died. There she was, a little bag of bones, a shadow of her former self. The adults ushered me out of the room. I went off and cried by myself. I never got to say good-bye. Later on, I found out that everyone knew she was dying, even before I went off to camp for two weeks. They didn't tell me about grandma. I felt betrayed. But what could I say or do? Everyone else was so sad. No one was interested in how I felt. So I kept it all in . . . to myself . . . until now."

The death of a beloved grandparent is a powerful event for any child. The impact is often lost in the sea of family grief. Children need to acknowledge and understand the death and to be able to go through the grieving process. It is best done with a parent.

That's why parents need to understand the depth of their child's attachment to a grandparent. And some children are so attached that they don't understand why a beloved grandparent is not with them all of the time. Younger children, especially, do not understand why a grandparent may live far away or in a nursing home. They don't understand where grandparents go when they die or why they die. They only know that they are not there anymore. (That's why cemeteries can be important emotional touchstones for children. A grave is seen as the physical place of a departed grandparent.)

When a close grandparent dies before the child has reached the age of reason (about age seven), the child never sees the grandparent grow old. Consequently, the grandparent is permanently frozen in the child's consciousness—immortalized. If the child never sees the grandparent die or never attends a funeral or memorial service, the grandparent lives, unchangingly, in the child's heart and spirit forever.

"My grandmother died when I was six years old," said Mackenzie, fourteen. "She is not really dead to me. I talk with her every night before I go to sleep. I discuss my day and ask her to help me. She is always sweet and smiling like she loves me so much. Like an angel."

Of course, the vitality of the grandparent who lives on in the child depends on the degree of intimacy that they shared. Some children who can't remember physical aspects or memories of events that are related to their grandparents nevertheless report "warm feelings" or "peace" when they see a picture of a grandparent who died before the child was seven years old. One child that I know wears his grandfather's red suspenders to this day. His grandfather was killed in a plane crash when the child was six years old. In fact, many children with this type of close relationship use the departed grandparent as a positive role model.

When a grandparent dies, it is important that we respect the repercussions of this event on the vital connection between our child and the grandparent. As deeply as we may be personally suffering, we must go the extra mile to give our child time to grieve, as well as grieve together. Lending an ear to what our child says and how she feels will bring us closer.

In most cases, the death of a grandparent is the first death a child experiences. So this process also serves as a rehearsal for future grieving and teaches the child to honor those who have passed, as well as to respect and appreciate those who are alive today. It makes our child appreciate *us* more. Expect also that the child may become more clingy, a bit frightened about losing us too. Reassurance helps.

Because death is part of life, there is no need to shelter children from the logistics involved (age appropriately, of course). Attending funerals and memorial services together, with parents, experiencing grief, talking about the grandparent, keeping a picture by the bedside, laughing about the good times, are all part of a healthy grieving process. Children should not be denied this experience, even by well-meaning parents who are trying to protect them from the pain. Children, as oracles, know exactly what is happening and need to participate in the process.

Death is an inevitable part of life. Hold hands when it happens.

I wish you well.

Notes

Introduction

1. I want to point out the difference between the terms *three-generational* and *three-dimensional*, as I use them here. Three-generational is a quantitative term that refers to biologically successive generations. I use three-dimensional to refer to a linear succession of generations that is extended in depth and breadth in a psychological, biological, social, emotional, intellectual, and spiritual way.

2. J.-P. Sartre, *The Words*, trans. B. Frechtman (New York: Fawcett, 1977), 14.

Chapter One

1. M. Mead, *Blackberry Winter* (New York: Morrow, 1972), 45.

2. A. Kornhaber and K. L. Woodward, *Grandparents/Grandchildren: The Vital Connection* (New York: Anchor Books, 1981), 164.

Chapter Six

1. A. Thomas, S. Chess, and H. Birch, *Temperament and Behavior Disorders in Children* (New York: New York University Press, 1968).

Chapter Nine

1. V. King and G. H. Elder, Jr., "Are Religious Grandparents More Involved Grandparents?" *Journal of Gerontology* 54, no. 6 (November 1999): 317–328.

2. A. Kornhaber, *The Grandparent Guide* (New York: Contemporary Books/McGraw-Hill, 2002), 280–293; C. J. Patterson, S. Hurt, and C. D. Mason, "Families of the Lesbian Baby Boom: Children's Contacts with Grandparents and Other Adults," *American Journal of Orthopsychiatry* 68, no. 3 (July 1998): 390–399.

Chapter Eleven

1. This letter was adapted and edited with permission from the Foundation for Grandparenting. It was adapted and published in the foundation's *Vital Connections* newsletter (fall/winter 1990) with permission from *CHADDER*, the magazine of the parents' organization for children with attention disorders (published in their fall 1989 edition). For more information about attention deficit disorder or CHADD, write to CHADD, 499 Northwest 70th Avenue, Suite 308, Plantation, Florida 33317, or call (305) 587-3700.

2. United States Department of Commerce, Bureau of the Census, *Living Arrangements of Children Under Eighteen Years Old, 1960 to Present* (Washington, D.C.: U.S. Government Printing Office, June 29, 2001). See www.census.gov.

3. J. F. Kennedy and V. T. Keeney, "The Extended Family Revisited: Grandparents Rearing Grandchildren," *Child Psychiatry and Human Development* 19 (1988): 26–35.

Suggested Reading

American Bar Association. *Grandparent Visitation Disputes* (Report no. 89-83439). Washington, D.C.: American Bar Association, 1989.

Areen, J. Statement before a hearing of the Subcommittee on Human Services, Select Committee on Aging, House of Representatives, Washington, D.C., December 1982.

Baranowski, M. D. "Grandparent Adolescent Relations: Beyond the Nuclear Family." *Adolescence* 15 (1982): 575–584.

Bekker, L. D., and Taylor, G. "Attitudes Toward the Aged in a Multigenerational Sample." *Journal of Gerontology* 21 (1996): 115–118.

Bengston, V. "Diversity and Symbolism in Grandparental Roles." In *Grandparenthood*, edited by V. Bengston and J. F. Robertson, 11–27. Thousand Oaks, Calif.: Sage, 1985.

Blackwelder, D. E., and Passman, R. E. "Grandmother's and Mother's Disciplining in Three-Generational Families." *Journal of Personality and Social Psychology* 50, no. 1 (1986): 80–86.

Blau, T. H. "An Evaluative Study of the Role of Grandparents in the Best Interest of the Child." *American Journal of Family Therapy* 12, no. 4 (1984): 47.

Bower, B. "Marked Questions on Elderly Depression." *Science News* 140, no. 20 (1991): 310–312.

Buchanan, B., and Lappin, J. "Restoring the Soul of the Family." *Family Therapy Networker* (November/December 1990): 46–52.

Burton, L. M. "Black Grandparents Rearing Children of Drug-Addicted Parents: Stressors, Outcomes, and Social Service Needs." *Gerontologist* 32, no. 6 (1992): 744–751.

Caren, L. D. "Effects of Exercise on the Human Immune System." *Bioscience* 41, no. 6 (1991): 410–416.

Cath, S. H. "Of Gifts and Grandfathering." Paper presented at the annual meeting of the American Gerontologic Society, Boston, May 1985.

Cerrato, P. L. "Does Diet Affect the Immune System?" *Registered Nurse* 53, no. 6 (1990): 67–70.

Chairman Reports. Subcommittee on Human Services, Select Committee on Aging, House of Representatives. *Grandparents: New Roles and Responsibilities* (Comm. pub. no. 102-876). Washington, D.C.: Subcommittee on Human Services, Select Committee on Aging, House of Representatives, 1992.

Cherlin, A., and Furstenberg, F., Jr. "Grandparents and Family Crisis." *Generations* 10, no. 4 (1986): 26–28.

Cherlin, A., and Furstenberg, F., Jr. *The New American Grandparent: A Place in the Family, a Life Apart*. New York: Basic Books, 1986.

Cloninger, C. R., Svrakic, D. M., and Pryzbeck, T. R. "A Psychobiological Model of Temperament and Character." *Archives of General Psychiatry* 50 (1993): 975–990.

Cohler, B. J. *Mothers, Grandmothers, and Daughters*. New York: Wiley, 1981.

Derdyn, A. P. "Grandparent Visitation Rights: Rendering Family Dissolution More Pronounced!" *American Journal of Orthopsychiatry* 55, no. 2 (April 1985): 27–28.

Drew, L. A., and Smith, P. K. "The Impact of Parental Separation/Divorce on Grandparent-Grandchild Relationships." *International Journal of Aging and Human Development* 8, no. 3 (1994): 191–216.

Erikson, E. H. *Childhood and Society*. New York: Norton, 1963, 173.

Erikson, E. H. *The Life Cycle Completed*. New York: Norton, 1982.

Erikson, E. H., Erikson, J. M., and Kivnick, H. *Vital Involvement in Old Age: The Experience of Old Age in Our Time*. New York: Norton, 1986.

Foster, R., and Freed, D. "Grandparent Visitation: Vagaries and Vicissitudes." *Journal of Divorce* 70, no. 1/2 (fall/winter 1979): 643–651.

Freedman, M. "Fostering Intergenerational Relationships for At-Risk Youths." *Children Today* 18, no. 2 (1989): 10–15.

Furstenberg, F., and Cherlin, A. *Divided Families*. Cambridge, Mass.: Harvard University Press, 1991.

Golden, R. N., and others. "Circulating Natural Killer Phenotypes in Men and Women with Major Depression: Relation to Catatonic Activity and Severity of Depression." *Archives of General Psychiatry* 49 (1992): 388–395.

Greenburg, J. S., and Becker, M. "Aging Parents as Family Resources." *Gerontologist* 28, no. 6 (1988): 786–791.

Hayslip, B. "Grandparents Raising Grandchildren: New Challenges for Geropsychologists." *Adult Development and Aging News* 5 (spring 2001).

Ivester, M. C., and King, K., eds. "Attitudes of Adolescents Toward the Aged." *Gerontologist* 17, no. 1 (1977): 22.

Jendrek, M. P. *Grandparents Who Parent Their Grandchildren*. Washington, D.C.: American Association of Retired Persons Report, 1993.

Johnson, C. "A Cultural Analysis of the Grandmother." *Research in Aging* 5, no. 4 (1983): 547–567.

Joseph, A. M., Jr. *The Indian Heritage of America*. New York: Bantam Books, 1968, 262.

Kennedy, J. F., and Keeney, V. T. "Group Psychotherapy with Grandparents Rearing Their Emotionally Disturbed Grandchildren." *Group* 11, no. 1 (1987): 15–25.

Kennedy, J. F., and Keeney, V. T. "The Extended Family Revisited: Grandparents Rearing Grandchildren." *Child Psychiatry and Human Development* 19 (1988): 26–35.

King, V., and Elder, G. H., Jr. "Are Religious Grandparents More Involved Grandparents?" *Journal of Gerontology* 54, no. 6 (November 1999): 317–328.

King v. King 8:28. S. W. 2d 630 (Ky). Cert. Denied 113. Ct. 378, 1992.

Kornhaber, A. "The Vital Connection Between the Old and the Young: The Birth of the Intergenerational Movement in America." Address presented at the national meeting of the Administration on Aging, Washington, D.C., October 1982.

Kornhaber, A. "Grandparents: The Other Victims of Divorce." *Reader's Digest*, February 1983.

Kornhaber, A. "Grandparents Are Coming of Age in America." *Children Today* 5, no. 2 (July 1983).

Kornhaber, A. "America's Forgotten Resource: Grandparents." *U.S. News and World Report*, June 1984.

Kornhaber, A. *Between Parents and Grandparents*. New York: St. Martin's Press, 1985.

Kornhaber, A. "The New Social Contract." In *Grandparenthood*, edited by V. Bengston and J. F. Robertson. Thousand Oaks, Calif.: Sage, 1985.

Kornhaber, A. "Grandparenting: Normal and Pathological." *American Journal of Geriatric Psychiatry* 7, no. 6 (1986).

Kornhaber, A. "Grandparents as Clinical Collaborators." *Vital Connections* 2, no. 2 (spring issue).

Kornhaber, A. "Grandfathers: From Warriors to Wise Men." Proceedings of the World Congress of Child Psychiatry, Paris, July 1986.

Kornhaber, A. "Are Your Children Problem Parents?" *Grandparents* 1, no. 2 (fall 1987).

Kornhaber, A. "What It Really Means to Grandparent." *Grandparents* 2, no. 2 (summer 1988).

Kornhaber, A. "Grandparents and Infants." *French Journal of Child Psychiatry* xvii, no. 2 (June 1989).

Kornhaber, A. "Infants and Grandparents." In *Infant Psychiatry*, edited by E. V. Rexford, L. W. Sander, and T. Shapiro. New Haven, Conn.: Yale University Press, 1989.

Kornhaber, A. *Spirit*. New York: St. Martin's Press, 1989.

Kornhaber, A. "Les Grands-Parents." In *Le Monde du Bebe*, edited by S. Lebovici and P. Weil-Halpern. Paris: Presse Medicale, 1990.

Kornhaber, A. "Talking to God." *Newsweek*, January 1992.

Kornhaber, A. "Raising Grandchildren." *Vital Connections* 14 (spring 1993).

Kornhaber, A. "The Grandparenting Instinct." Foundation for Grandparenting Web site. (www.grandparenting.org). August 2001.

Kornhaber, A., and Woodward, K. L. "Bringing Back Grandma." *Newsweek*, May 1981.

Kornhaber, A., and Woodward, K. L. *Grandparents/Grandchildren: The Vital Connection*. New York: Anchor Books, 1981, 164–168.

Kornhaber, A., and Woodward, K. L. *Grands-Parents, Petits-Enfants: Le Lien Vital*. Paris: Robert Laffont, 1985.

Lowinsky, N. R. *Stories from the Motherline*. Los Angeles: Tarcher, 1996.

Matthews, S. H., and Sprey, J. "The Impact of Divorce on Grandparenthood: An Exploratory Study." *Gerontologist* 24 (February 1984): 41–47.

McGoldrick, J. P., and Giordano, N., eds. *Ethnicity and Family Therapy*. New York: Guilford Press, 84–107.

McGreal, C. E. "The Birth of the First Grandchild: A Longitudinal Study of the Transition to Grandparenthood." *Dissertation Abstract International* 46, no. 02 (1985): 675B.

Minkler, M., and Roe, K. *Grandmothers as Caregivers*. Thousand Oaks, Calif.: Sage, 1993.

Minkler, M., and Fuller-Thomson, E. "The Health of Grandparents Raising Grandchildren: Results of a National Study." *American Journal of Public Health* 89, no. 9 (September 1999): 1384–1389.

Oliver, J. E. "Intergenerational Transmission of Child Abuse: Rates, Research, and Clinical Implications." *American Journal of Psychiatry* 150 (1993): 1315–1324.

Pashos, A. "Grandparental Solicitude." *PubMed* (PMID 10785346). Hamburg, Germany: Institute of Human Biology, University of Hamburg, 2000.

Patterson, C. J., Hurt, S., and Mason, C. D. "Families of the Lesbian Baby Boom: Children's Contacts with Grandparents and Other Adults." *American Journal of Orthopsychiatry* 68, no. 3 (July 1998): 390–399.

Pearson, B. "Child Custody: Why Not Let the Parents Decide?" *Judges Journal* 20 (1981): 4.

Peterson, C. C. "Grandmothers and Grandfathers Satisfaction with the Grandparenting Roles." *International Journal of Aging and Human Development* 49, no. 1 (1999): 61–68.

Roberto, K. A., and Stroes, J. "Children and Grandparents: Roles, Influences, and Relationships." *International Journal of Aging and Human Development* 34, no. 3 (1992): 228.

Saltzman, G. A. "Grandparents Raising Grandchildren." *Creative Grandparenting, Inc.* 2, no. 4 (1992).

Somary, K., and Stricker, G. "Becoming a Grandparent: A Longitudinal Study of Expectations and Early Experiences as a Function of Sex and Lineage." *Gerontologist* 38, no. 1 (February 1998): 53–61.

Spruyette, N., and others. "Grandparents: The Experience of the Relationship with the Oldest Grandchild and Their Psychological Well-Being." *Tijdschr Gerontoligica Geriatrica* 30, no. 1 (February 1999): 21–30.

Stone, E. "Mothers and Daughters." *Parents Magazine* 66, no. 5 (1991): 83–87.

Stotland, L. N. "Gender-Based Biology." *American Journal of Psychiatry* 158, no. 2 (February 2001): 161–162.

Strom, R., and Strom, S. *Becoming a Better Grandparent*. Thousand Oaks, Calif.: Sage, 1991.

Strom, R., and Strom, S. *Achieving Grandparent Potential*. Thousand Oaks, Calif.: Sage, 1992.

Thomas, A., Chess, S., Birch, H. *Temperament and Behavior Disorders in Children*. New York: New York University Press, 1968.

Timberlake, E. M., and Chipungu, S. "Grandmotherhood: Contemporary Meaning Among African American Middle Class Grandmothers." *Social Work* 37, no. 3 (1992): 216–222.

Turtletaub, S. *The Grandfather Thing*. Los Angeles: Tallfellow Press, 2001, 10.

United States Department of Commerce, Bureau of the Census. *Statistical Abstract of the United States*. Washington, D.C.: U.S. Government Printing Office, 1990.

United States Department of Commerce, Bureau of the Census. *Living Arrangements of Children Under Eighteen Years Old, 1960 to Present*. Washington, D.C.: U.S. Government Printing Office, June 29, 2001.

U.S. Department of Health and Human Services. *Births, Marriages, Divorces, and Deaths for January–December 2000* (National Vital Statistics Report 49, no. 6). Washington, D.C.: U.S. Government Printing Office, 2001.

Victor, R. S. Statement before a hearing of the Subcommittee on Human Services, Select Committee on Aging, House of Representatives, Washington, D.C., December 1982.

Wiscott, R., and Kopera-Frye, K. "Sharing of Cultures: Adult Grandchildren's Perceptions of Intergenerational Relations." *International Journal of Aging and Human Development* 51, no. 3 (2000): 199–215.

Resources

The following are some useful resources for parents and grandparents.

Adolescence

Your Adolescent: Emotional, Behavioral, and Cognitive Development from Early Adolescence Through the Teen Years, by D. Pruitt and the American Academy of Child and Adolescent Psychiatry, New York: HarperCollins, 2000.

Adoption

Adoptive Families of America, Inc.
3333 Highway 100 N
Minneapolis, Minnesota 55422
(612) 535-4829

Generations of Hope
1530 Fairway Drive
Rantoul, Illinois 61866
(217) 893-4673
http://www.hope4children.org/index.htm.

National Adoption Information Clearinghouse
11426 Rockville Pike, Suite 410
Rockville, Maryland 20852
(301) 984-8527

Disabilities

National Information Center for Youth with Disabilities
P.O. Box 1492
Washington, D.C. 20013-1492
(800) 695-0285

Parent Network
500 Balltown Road
Schenectady, New York 12304
(800) 305-8817

Diversity

Human Rights Campaign
919 Eighteenth Street NW, Suite 800
Washington, D.C. 20006
(202) 628-4160
http://www.hrc.org

Just for Us
Sons and Daughters of Gays and Lesbians
c/o Colage
3023 N. Clark, Box 121
Chicago, Illinois 60657

Parents, Families, and Friends of Lesbians and Gays (PFLAG)
1726 M Street NW, Suite 400
Washington, D.C. 20036
(202) 467-8180
http://www.pflag.com

Teaching Tolerance Project
Southern Poverty Law Center
http://www.splcenter.org/teachingtolerance/tt-index.html

Divorce

Divorce Anonymous
2600 Colorado Avenue, Suite 270
Santa Monica, California 90404
(310) 998-6538

New Beginnings, Inc.
13129 Clifton Road
Silver Springs, Maryland 20904
(301) 384-0111

Grandparenting

The Foundation for Grandparenting
http://www.grandparenting.org
The Grandparent Guide, by A. Kornhaber, New York: Contemporary
    Books/McGraw-Hill, 2002

Raising Grandchildren

AARP Grandparent Information Center
601 E Street NW
Washington, D.C. 20049
(202) 434-2296
http://www.aarp.org

Generations United
122 C Street NW, Suite 820
Washington, D.C. 20001
(202) 638-1263
http://www.gu.org

Stepfamilies

Stepfamily Association of America
215 Centennial Mall South, Suite 212
Lincoln, Nebraska 68508
(800) 735-0329

The Stepfamily Foundation
333 West End Avenue
New York, New York 10023
(212) 877-3244
http://www.stepfamily.org

About the Author

Arthur Kornhaber, M.D., is a grandfather, clinician, researcher, medical writer, and the founder and president of the Foundation for Grandparenting. A leading authority on the relationship between parents, grandparents, and grandchildren, he is the author of six internationally recognized books and numerous articles on the topic. Dr. Kornhaber is a life fellow of the American Academy of Child and Adolescent Psychiatry and a life member of the American Medical Association and the American Psychiatric Association. He writes articles, speaks widely, and appears regularly in the media, including on the network morning shows (NBC, CBS, and so forth), to raise family consciousness and to educate people about family-related issues. He directs the Foundation for Grandparenting Web site, www.grandparenting.org.

Index